Finding the
Quiet Mind

Books by Robert Ellwood

Alternative Altars

Religious and Spiritual
Groups in Modern America

Mysticism and Religion

Many Peoples, Many Faiths

Finding Deep Joy

Theosophy

Cover art by *Jane A. Evans*

Finding the Quiet Mind

ROBERT ELLWOOD

*This publication made possible with
the assistance of the Kern Foundation*

The Theosophical Publishing House
Wheaton, Ill. U.S.A.
Madras, India / London, England

The Theosophical Publishing House,
306 West Geneva Road,
Wheaton, Illinois 60189.

Published by the Theosophical Publishing House,
a department of the Theosophical Society
in America.

Library of Congress Cataloging in
Publication Data:
Ellwood, Robert S., 1933-
  Finding the quiet mind.

  "A Quest book"
  1. Meditation.   I. Title
BL627.E44   1983   158'.12   83-615
ISBN 0-8356-0576-0 (pbk.)

Printed in the United States of America

For *Gracia Fay*, and for my students, whose experiences helped make this book possible.

Contents

vii

Preface

If you are interested in calming your mind and reaching inner resources of joy and power for daily living, but are not too concerned about exotic-seeming schools and techniques of meditation, then you are the sort of person for whom *Finding the Quiet Mind* is intended. In writing this guide to meditation, I have drawn from teaching experience and from a wide range of material Eastern and Western. I have endeavored to bring it all together into a coherent synthesis and put it into contemporary language for the modern reader.

Two basic premises underlie this approach. First, I assume that the effective practice of meditation to benefit one's everyday life does not depend on any particular philosophical belief. It can fit nicely into different worldviews—religious, seeking, or secular—so long as one is open to meditation and the self-discovery it entails. Second, I presuppose that, with the help of a book like this one, most people can make headway with meditation independently, without necessarily having an external teacher. Many, I think, would really rather work at it on their own, and for them this book is written. Some cautions are in order and have been expressed in the book. But on the whole I think too much has been made of meditation as a precarious practice requiring constant guidance. Whether or not one reaches the ultimate heights of spirituality, I have no doubt that a normal person in reasonably good mental health—the sort of person for whom this book is written—can practice the basic, unassuming kinds of meditation here described with considerable benefit. May you find your life enriched!

1

Stop the Action

It's been called the Monkey Mind.

It's that stream of consciousness which keeps flitting from one thing to another like a monkey jumping from branch to branch.

Within the course of a single hour, your mind will concentrate for a little while on what you're doing—reading, sewing, working, watching TV, whatever it is. Then it will drift off to fantasize about something you did yesterday or are going to do next weekend, or to daydream about someone you met a year ago. You'll get hungry or thirsty and that sharp physical need will gnaw at you until it's satisfied or, if that's impossible at the moment, you put it down with a firm act of the will. You feel a harsh twinge of anxiety, even nausea, as something reminds you of an unresolved problem you have or a difficult appointment tomorrow. And so it goes.

The play of the Monkey Mind is not all bad. Some of it is and some of it isn't. But it all adds up to one thing: You're not in charge. You're not thinking. Your thoughts are thinking you. And they in turn are slave to whatever cherries or lemons the slot machine of the world happens to turn up. Externally, the machine flashes up all sorts of beckoning objects to want, thrills to seek, goals to pursue. Within, the mighty organ of the emotions plays symphonies—often discordant—with your appetites, memories, daydreams, moods, feelings, angers, fears, joys. Unchained in this monkey paradise, the beast has to jump very fast indeed to keep up with the whirling wheels and the raucous music.

And the Monkey Mind can't stop by itself.

Then there's the Sloth Mind. Sometimes the Monkey Mind does seem to slow down, but the result is not much better. In fact it may be a lot worse, so much so that you deliberately try to run around and stimulate the Monkey Mind into as frenetic a pace as possible to keep the Other Thing from having a chance to break in. That Other Thing, the Sloth Mind, is pervasive anxiety and depression. It's when you can't shake that clammy, jittery feel in the hands and that haunting fear something bad is about to happen, when you just can't seem to stop thinking about the things that worry you—they keep popping back up in the mind like werewolf jack-in-the-boxes. You may not even know what you're anxious or depressed about, you just are. It may get so bad you go to bed.

Blaise Pascal wrote that the human condition is one of "inconstancy, boredom, and anxiety," and more recently Lewis Thomas in *The Medusa and the Snail* wrote that while we humans are "a spectacular, splendid manifestation of life," with language, affection, and music, also

> We are, perhaps, uniquely among the earth's creatures, the worrying animal. We worry away our lives, fearing the future, discontent with the present, unable to take in the idea of dying, unable to sit still.

When the Sloth Mind is hard upon us, that's the aspect of human nature which crawls to the front and sits there sullenly, unwilling to move aside. You don't know why; like mornings when there's fog, it's simply there.

Finally there's the Cow Mind. It just wants to chew its cud and not be bothered. Perhaps you've struck a compromise between the Monkey Mind and the Sloth Mind. You're neither too up nor too down. You don't expect too much from life and you've built walls around yourself to keep out the bad things. You don't give, you don't get, you just get along. You coast through your work as best you can, then you eat, read the sports page or a lightweight magazine, watch TV and smoke, then go to bed.

If you have a family you spend some time with them but don't let them get to you too much. The next day you do it all over again. You don't know why you're living but you don't want to die, mainly because you don't want to get sick and because you don't want anything as dramatic as dying to happen to you. Maybe the Cow Mind is o.k. so long as nothing big like divorce or dying happens, and so long as you're content with gray and don't especially want a rainbow full of colors.

Suppose you want to shoot the Monkey, liven up the Sloth, or kick some life into the Cow. Many, many people don't like who they are and try all sorts of ways to switch.

Some drink or take drugs. On a more salutary plane, some jog, some write, some make love, some labor for good causes. Some combine several of these.

Another antidote is meditation.

Meditation may not be for everyone. If you really try it and it doesn't seem to work for you, that doesn't mean there's something wrong with you. You have nothing to worry about or feel guilty about. You'll just have to find another way to get your mind in harness, that's all.

But if you want to give meditation a fair trial, be sure a fair trial is what it is. Read this book. Work at it, and don't give up too soon. Don't expect too much or too little from meditation. Go about it in the right way and with the right attitudes. If you need to change your style of life and your values to make them compatible with seriously practicing meditation, do so. Otherwise the trial is bound to fail.

It's like learning any new skill. The first few tries will often be disappointing and the temptation to quit will push itself forward persistently. But I have known very few persons who could not reach a satisfying level of ability in meditation with enough perseverance.

It is important to realize exactly what meditation can and cannot do. Here at the outset, let us emphasize that meditation is not a psychological cure-all. It will not solve serious mental problems and its practice by persons with real mental illness may do more harm than good. People who think they may have a definite mental health or emotional difficulty should seek assistance from trained helpers. Meditation is not magic, and will not magically remove the causes of anxiety, depression, or lethargy. It will not remove temptations and distractions, pay the bills or solve family problems.

What it can do is affect the way the mind works so that it responds differently than before to these things—with more calmness, with greater access to reservoirs of inner joy and strength. This means being less distracted by the Monkey, less bogged down by the Sloth, less out of it than the Cow.

Meditation is a counterweight within oneself to all those things. It matches the way they sap one with new inflows of peace, energy, and happiness, for meditation can touch and tap a place accessible to the Quiet Mind, the mind just being itself, from which those positive powers flow.

Many people may want some of these good things, but are not sure they want to meditate, or even that they can. Here are some common reasons for rejecting the practice.

"Meditation is too exotic. It comes from alien religions and cultures that are not my own and I would feel strange, even disloyal, if I got into it."

"Meditation is really for religious specialists, like monks and nuns. For someone like me to get involved in it would be going in a little too deep. I'd be over my head, and probably either couldn't handle it, or would become a religious nut."

"It's too difficult and technical. I've seen some books on meditation that made it sound like organizing a mission to Mars."

"It takes too much self-discipline. I don't like feeling I have to do anything more than the bare minimum on a regular basis. I'm a hang-loose kind of person who would rather just let it happen spontaneously."

"Meditation is just a kind of self-hypnosis. It's a deceptive trick you play on yourself, making yourself believe things are all right when really nothing has changed. I'd rather just have my honest ups and downs."

"Meditation is a self-centered escape from the real problems of the world. It doesn't feed the hungry, heal the sick, or solve the great political, ecological, or scientific problems we have. It's just spiritual self-indulgence."

During the course of this book we will answer these objections, and perhaps some others as well.

We will see that practices like meditation have been known in virtually every culture and religion, Eastern and Western. It is the rightful heritage of every human being.

Moreover, we will see that although meditation can be made to sound very difficult and "advanced," appropriate only to monastics and holy men living in caves, this attitude is one-sided at the least and almost criminal if it discourages any "ordinary" person from seeking its benefits. For the fact is that while there are more and less complicated techniques for inducing the mind into the meditative state, and for superimposing religious meaning on it, the essence of meditation is amazingly simple.

It is so simple, in fact, that one who came to meditation thinking it was some "big deal" might feel a touch of disappointment until he or she was able to realize that simplicity is precisely the point. It is gearing the wheels of thought down to a much lower, simpler ratio than we are used to. It is letting the waves of the mind settle down, and nothing is simpler than a clear, still, deep pond. It is so uncomplex that it would be impossible for it to accomplish anything as tricky as self-deception, unless that's what you want it to do, or what you want to think it's doing.

It is true that meditation takes some self-discipline, some work. But if that idea throws you, ask yourself if you don't really want a little more self-discipline. People without self-discipline are not really happy. They are the ones who never accomplish anything and are always at the mercy of the Monkey, Sloth, and Cow Minds. Maybe what you need is something in your life that will tighten the screws of self-discipline a few notches.

But on the other hand, beginning meditation doesn't mean you're going to have to start living like a monk in some austere order. A good meditation need not take longer than a good shower. It can be as regular, and can slip as unobtrusively into your daily regimen, as bathing or brushing your teeth. It's true, as we shall see, that meditation practice ought to have an effect on your lifestyle as well, but it doesn't mean you have to wear sandals (unless you want to) or a hair shirt. It just means getting all the facets of your life together.

Finally, let us dispel the notion there is anything escapist, unworldly, or non-problem-solving about meditation. Meditation makes people calmer and happier. Calm and happy people see things as they are and are good at solving real problems.

Of course, anything, including meditation, can be used as a crutch and an escape. But is is harder to do this with meditation than with Monkey Mind stuff, or with the crutch and escape of ordinary habits and hobbies. That is because meditation at least forces you to be alone with yourself and face yourself, not the favorite pastime of your ordinary escapist. On the contrary, history is full of persons from the Buddha to Gandhi and Mother Teresa who were both great accomplishers and great meditators, and who

left more of a mark for good in the world
than thousands of more "practical" people.

In this book we will stick to the
simplicities of meditation, dealing with it as
something as plain as an ironing board and
as everyday and natural as eating breakfast.
It will not be promoted as religious, as salvation or enlightenment. It will not be viewed
as some great mystical glory-road that will
expand your consciousness out to Neptune
or teach you the secrets of the ages. Some
meditators think of meditation as a way of
getting in touch with the Reality behind
religion and so see it as part of their spiritual
life. That is all right. Others prefer to think
of it chiefly in terms of its psychological
value here and now, on a one reality or one-
world-at-a-time basis. That is all right, too.
   Birds presumably never think about the
nature of air or of flying, nor fish of the
nature of water and swimming. But con-
ceivably a diving bird who occasionally

plunges out of the air to swim, or a flying fish who sometimes glides through the alien element of air, would think about air and water, swimming and flying. In the same way, though you may usually not bother to think about what consciousness is, or even what life is, you may find when you start meditating and dive or leap—however you want to put it—into other ways of experiencing consciousness and life, you start to wonder what they're all about, what mind and life really are. But though meditation may start you thinking, the value of meditation does not depend on your having any one right answer to the big questions.

The important thing is that debates, whether within ourselves or with others, about the metaphysical meaning of meditation should not be allowed to stand in the way of actually doing it and letting it improve our life. Like all such, these philosophical disputations are quibbles about words and concepts, not the thing itself. Better to do meditation and let it speak for itself about its meaning and value.

In our approach, the basic fact about meditation is that it is just the Quiet Mind. It is the mind taking a little time out just to be itself, to step outside the games of life and find out what it is when it is not preoccupied with Monkey, Sloth, or Cow business, when it is *just itself*. My experience and that of many others is that, when this time out is allowed, remarkable things can happen to the mind that deepen, recharge, and refresh.

Here are a couple of accounts of experiences in a meditation experiment in a university class I taught some years ago. For the most part the students had not meditated before. We talked briefly about various methods, such as counting breaths, then allowed fifteen minutes for the exercise: afterwards the students anonymously wrote up what transpired. For example:

> That was the fastest fifteen minutes I've ever consciously experienced! My body relaxed almost immediately (that posture really works!). I began to concentrate on my breathing. I didn't *start out* counting my breaths, but that's what it gradually evolved

to anyway from just concentrating on them. I began to count in rhythm—one, two, three, etc., all the way to ten and then I started over. I found that even when my mind strayed (it did that quite a few times—for instance a fellow behind me couldn't seem to control his giggles, which was quite distracting at first) *anyway*—even when my mind strayed, I found myself still counting my breaths—never missing a count all the way through a distraction. Eventually my mind seemed to detach itself just a few inches above my body. I was aware of a numbness in my body.

When I opened my eyes—things somehow seemed a bit different than from what they had been when I closed them (desks, chairs, people, etc.). Oh!—I just remember—at one point I felt so *good*—a surge of sort of "euphoric bliss" welled up for an *instant*. I felt like laughing out loud, but I didn't. And then the feeling went away.

And another student:

Originally, I became very conscious of breathing, sounds, pulses, etc., within me. I found sight to be distracting and found images on the inside of my mind to be much more unique. Throughout I tried not to notice voices and sounds but only after some period did they not distract me (although I was vaguely aware). I felt as though I were inside my mind. I desired experience. Coolness, mellowness, and calm approached me. I felt as though I were in a cave trying to push myself back into the darkness away from sight, sound, and especially time. My mind kept wanting to move the body position, but after a short period forgot about it. The experiences were few, but very real. My mind persisted in distorting everything to irrelevant thought. At the close, I found myself very unconcerned with things that had been troubling me.

These accounts represent only novice, experimental meditations. With repetition, they could become smoother, less ego-involved, perhaps more deeply joyous. At the same time, we must not forget that moments, indeed often severe crises of distraction, self-preoccupation, and dryness will dog even the most experienced meditator. Like any great art, meditation is always a struggle yet always rewarding. It seems sometimes hopelessly futile and sometimes so supremely worthwhile as to make everything else in life seem futile by comparison.

These narratives nonetheless display several basic characteristics of meditation. We see a change in the ordinary experience of space and time. Time may seem to the meditator to run faster (or slower) than usual, and he or she may have a sense of "lightness," even of floating in space. Awareness of the automatic body functions, such as breathing, heart, pulse, may be heightened. One may "see" the activity of the mind as though watching its parade of thoughts and attentions like a movie on a screen, as though there were a Watcher within one's own brain. As the meditation deepens, a joyous calm may spread, then sharpen into ecstasy. Finally, coming out, somehow one knows he or she has been Somewhere Else and undergone a sea change: things look different, he feels different, problems aren't what they were when he went in.

All that really happened, though, was that for the fifteen minutes, or whatever it was, he found a different way of being a consciousness in this world. Ordinarily our consciousness is mostly concerned with the outer things that impinge upon us through sense data, or with their inner reflections in our thinking, emotions, and memories. Now, in meditation, consciousness deliberately tries to disengage from all that and just be itself as itself, sheer consciousness. Unsupported mind. The mind being what it is when it is not thinking about anything in particular, nor asleep, nor lethargic, nor stoned. Simply clear, bright, alert, an unstained mirror, enjoying itself just as consciousness, the way a runner enjoys himself simply as a lively, responsive, healthy physical organism.

When the mind is enjoying being itself and not worrying, a lot of things will shake themselves out on their own. Many problems take care of themselves without worry as well as with worry.

Another value is that as the mind leaps up to become the Watcher it sees the panorama of its activity from a higher perspective. It sees itself in the automatic functions of the body and the ever-flowing almost automatic stream of consciousness. Seeing all of this from above, the mind gets a better idea than before of how it works, as well as the valuable realization that it doesn't *have* to be identified with the bodily functions and the stream of consciousness.

Most important of all, in due time those identifications of mind become unconscious, and the meditator's mind becomes the Quiet Mind. Then it gets a chance for deep relaxation and can come out powerfully recharged. Some studies have suggested that a half-hour of deep meditation can have the reinvigorating effect of several hours of sleep;

many meditators comment most on the refreshing effect of their practice. If you want to go on to affirm that the Quiet Mind has moved into life-giving conjunction with God or Ultimate Reality, or is realizing its identity on the deepest level with that transcendent Source of its being, that is fine too.

What then is meditation? Linguistically, the root of this Latin-derived word is related to words as diverse as middle, mediation, medical, and measure; its ancient root also has overtones of pondering and reflecting. What all this comes to is a medicine for the mind which does its work by measuring out time, when it can reach a median, a point of equilibrium. Here the mind balances off its conflicting claims and enjoys a therapeutic rest just being itself. Meditation is a wholesome stopping of the action.

This is revitalizing, preparing the meditator to mend the world and his or her own life with greater effect. It strikes at the world's ills at some level near to their deepest and most stubborn root. Pascal once remarked, "I have discovered that all human evil comes from this, man's being unable to sit still in a room." He meant, presumably, men with no love for the Quiet Mind; those who have it can sit with a deep and wonderful stillness, doing no harm, then arise to move into the world, calm and bearing effective good.

The conception of meditation as the Quiet Mind, the Mind at Rest, is different, to be sure, from some ideas of meditation. For many people meditation means thinking beautiful, inspirational thoughts, or thinking deeply on sacred truths. In certain Western spiritual traditions, meditation is thought of mainly as visualizing scriptural or other religious scenes, then discerning inwardly their meaning and application. But many of these same teachers tell us that sometimes it moves by grace from these active visualizations and cogitations into an even higher activity, contemplation, or the simple, formless enjoyment of God's love and presence.

As noted before, words in themselves are not the thing; whether one prefers to call what we have spoken of as the Quiet Mind *meditation* or *contemplation* or something else should not be a source of friction. I shall later discuss the value of visualization as preparation for entering the Quiet Mind. But, following common usage today, I will use the word *meditation* to include the formless, contemplative reaches, too.

For I feel that the latter should be considered common and accessible, not some rare cloisterish gift. Undoubtedly there are exceptional levels of meditation which only great saints have attained, but that is not our concern at the moment. Like most of the great saints themselves, let us turn our gaze from the exotic flora and fauna of mysticism to the task of helping everyone, even mere beginners, raise the general level of inner life. That means finding for ourselves and others the Quiet Mind, in which even the holiest mental labor is hushed for a moment.

2

Getting Ready

Two of the most important sentences ever uttered are these: "Know yourself," the inscription over the portal of the temple at Delphi in ancient Greece, and the words of Jesus, "You must be born again." Any human being who completed the assignments contained in these two commandments would be a marvelously changed person, as different from the ordinary run as high noon from the first rosy fingers of dawn.

Meditation is a royal road that can carry one a long way toward both ends. In meditation much will be unveiled about the self and how it works, what its secret joys and troubles are; and much can be untangled about one's life. The experience parallels the pangs and victory of childbirth, and one can end up a fresh person.

But without hope, without expectation, nothing will come of meditation practice. The first requirement for successful meditation, then, is *to be eager for—and prepared for—important new self-knowledge and important change.*

Many of us do not really want to know ourselves. We are more afraid than intrigued by what we might find if we looked very deep beneath the surface. When the Monkey Mind is running wild, we're too distracted by the surface pleasures and pains to look much further. We think—as the Monkey wants us to—that we're one-dimensional and what we see on the surface is what we are. If the thought occurs of peering further in, we shunt it aside for fear that this would slow the Monkey down, and he's all the fun we know.

When the Sloth Mind takes over, we don't want to look inward because our overriding fear is that we'll just find gunk—deeper, heavier, and thicker gunk. For the Cow Mind, obviously really knowing oneself is the last thing to be desired, for any hint that the Cow way of life is stifling would upset its delicate but sluggish equilibrium between ignorance and inertia.

I can assure you that if, through meditation or otherwise, you learn more about yourself, you will discover realms far other than the Monkey, Sloth, and Cow layers that encrust the mind's surface. Some will probably be beautiful and some terrifying. You may have had hints of them in dreams. But exploring them will give you adventures entirely worth having. More I cannot tell you now. You must want to find them, and then find them for yourself.

One thing you will find is that meditation will have complex interactions with the rest of your life. It will not have magical, instantaneous effects, but it will permeate through your attitudes and instinctive responses. You will not necessarily end up a saint—at least right off—but you will likely find that somehow you handle the ordinary hurdles of daily life a little better. Here, for example, is the account of a woman university student during her first few days of meditating.

Thursday, 10/22, 8 p.m.

Well, that was certainly harder than I thought it would be. I had to force myself to sit in a progressively more uncomfortable position for twenty minutes. Oh! What an eternity that twenty minutes was! And my mind just would not let *go*. It kept insisting I think of what I would write down when I completed sitting. I finally turned off all the lights, lit a candle and counted out loud while concentrating on the flame of the candle.

This definitely was an improvement as it made me unaware of the pain in my legs and helped to clear my mind of all intruding thoughts. However, I was certainly glad when the twenty minutes were over and I could go cook my dinner. I don't think this particular sitting will have any beneficial effect on my life, but I am optimistic—they can only get better!

Friday, 10/23, 7:30 p.m.

I was very much looking forward to practicing tonight and got to it immediately upon returning home from work. I had had a long, tiring day, needed to relax and wanted to see if there was some improvement over last night's disastrous attempt. My optimism paid off for it was a very rewarding experience. I was able (for the most part) to obliterate everything from my mind, and just concentrate on my breathing and the candle. I found my thoughts drifting occasionally to my boyfriend who was due to arrive in an hour, but they weren't unpleasant interruptions and I was easily able to return to counting my breaths. I think that I tried too hard last night. I find that if *I* am relaxed in my attitude it is much easier. The time went by so fast I could not believe it. I actually would not have minded sitting a little longer—I was thoroughly enjoying the peace and tranquillity I had found. I now feel very refreshed and ready for a night on the town, almost as if I had just taken a long, leisurely soak in the tub. Set me loose—I've got a smile on my heart that is bursting in want of sharing it with someone!

Saturday, 10/24, 10 p.m.

I practiced tonight at my boyfriend's house, kind of a weird sensation as I could just feel him snickering in the other room. But I stuck out my twenty minutes and it was his loss (he wouldn't join me) and my gain as I feel terrific once again upon completion. Last night's sitting was far better than tonight's. I did not concentrate as well (TV in the other room? or lack of candle?) and my back began to get a little sore. I did notice that I was unusually patient today with my roommate's boyfriend who has taken up a quasi-residence in my apartment. I tolerated

[him] and even calmed down my boyfriend who was within three words of bodily removing him from my living room. I also found that I could relate to people a little better. I had a marvelous relaxed dinner with my boyfriend's parents. I was much more relaxed and natural in conversation and behavior. It seemed as though I was very "accepting" of the entire situation—of me, of his parents, of him, of the conversation, of everything. I am very satisfied with everything, I guess.

Sunday, 10/25, 6 p.m.

Got off work early and came home to an empty apartment, so I decided to sit a little early. I find that returning to the candle helps my concentration immensely. Tonight I tried to really focus on how I felt, my bodily sensations, during meditation. I have a feeling that I am not supposed to feel as I do—as if I were in a pseudo-dreamy state, almost as if I had just awakened in the morning. I love to sit and meditate. I find myself really looking forward to it each evening as it offers such a release from the tensions of the day ... Tonight when I rose from sitting I felt very disoriented, almost as if I were not in the room, not in my body, but looking down on the entire scene from a corner of the room. I liked the sensation. It was a nice "floaty" feeling, kind of like falling asleep in a lover's arms in front of a nice warm fireplace—very comforting and cozy. Practicing has done wonders for my relationship with my boyfriend. Nothing rattles or upsets me as it would have four days ago. . . . I don't know if meditation is the thing to credit for my good mood, but if it is I am thankful.

Sunday, 10/25, 11 p.m.

Well, my good mood was short-lived, as was having the apartment to myself for once. Good God, that man can set my nerves on fire. I couldn't sleep, I have anxiety bottled up from my toes to the hair on my head, so I decided to put meditation to a little use and see if it could help me relax. Forcing myself to concentrate on something other than my feelings (i.e., the candle) did help to some extent. At least I don't feel like sending him on a kamikaze mission anymore. In fact, I found sitting such an excellent escape that I sat for a full half hour without even flinching. Well, meditation, I guess you are good for something after all!

Monday, 10/26, 8 p.m.

No practice tonight—off to bed with the flu.

The jerky but appreciable growth in meditation practice, and measurable impact meditation seemed to have on daily life, mood, and interpersonal relations is evident in this account. Of course, just as the flu can really inhibit meditation, so can other distractions from "outside life," especially if one does not know to handle them within meditation. Another woman student, after several successful days of beginning meditation, reported this:

Friday

I've been starting to look forward to my meditation, but today was a bad experience because a very close friend of mine was hurt badly. When I sat down to meditation, all I could think of was him, and if he was in much pain, so I gave up after ten minutes. It was upsetting because I was finally starting to get a stronger concentration...

Saturday

This has been awful because my meditation efforts have gone back to the very beginning with the pain in the legs and the wandering mind. Ever since my friend was hurt, all I could think of was his recovery.

She apparently has not yet realized that sad events like this can be a motivation to good meditation as well as a distraction. One can try to make meditation a positive force in the situation. The young woman could have attempted "sending" out light and peace to the injured person in meditation, rather than just worrying about him. Some meditators, in fact, use the thought and image of a person important to them as the focus of meditation. Whether that person is a source of strength or in need, his or her mental picture serves to hold concentration and channel mental energy.

In both examples, though, the point is clear that meditation and the rest of life interact. Events in one have consequences in the other. If you begin meditating, things will become different in the remainder of your life—and the quality of your meditation will depend in no small part on how that rest of your life impinges on meditation. Whether your life is supportive or at odds with good meditation practice, and whether or not you manage constructively in meditation, the inescapable bad things out there can make a crucial difference. Even if all you do is turn to meditation instead of blowing up when the tension gets too great, and grudgingly hold your peace with someone you otherwise would like to send to hell in a handbasket, that is something.

Let's consider the way in which overall lifestyle affects meditation and may need to be changed for effective meditation. Most lives as they are ordinarily lived are elaborate compromises. They are complicated balance-of-power games that would do credit to the most astute diplomat. We may more than suspect that the veneer of Monkey Mind, Sloth Mind, and Cow Mind plasters over a mess that really ought to be flushed out. On the other hand, we live well-honed lives before lots of onlookers who accept us as we are, and nobody wants to reveal the junk before the unavoidable gaze of such an audience. We may, like Paul the Apostle, do things we would not, think thoughts we would not, have dark moods we would not, and somehow miss the joy we would have. But that only makes us like everyone else, and who wants to be too different?

We keep our principles propped up but only just enough to avoid completely overshadowing our appetites and desires for comfort, which will not keep still. We keep self and others on two ends of a seesaw. We take pleasures where we can, but not so eagerly as to upset work, family, and familiar routine. Keeping things hassle-free is commonly preferred over the possibilities of spectacular, but probably complicated and tiring, raptures. So it goes. We get by. That's life. Why should I want a big change?

No reason. It's your life. It's up to you. But if you really want to shake out and shape up a few things and do it through trying meditation—which is likely to entail fewer bills due later than a binge or an affair—remember that a compromise house-of-cards life with a lot of strains and wobbles will make your meditation wobbly too.

True, sooner or later your meditation may influence your lifestyle for good. But don't wait for that to happen: get your house in order as you begin meditation, or even before, to save painful stress and tension. The point is this. Meditation calms down, pacifies the mind. It brings in a state which is profoundly nonangry, nonantagonistic to other persons and one's environment; which is in a position of poise, strength, and peace toward the universe.

If the rest of your life is the opposite of this, if you are often riled up, if you are angry a lot of the time or depressed, if your life is chaotic and you are pulled this way and that with appetites, desires, giving in to pressure from others, just living at a hectic pace and a helter-skelter agenda, the clash between that turmoil and your meditation will be titanic. A gulf like the Grand Canyon will loom. This can't be any good. You'll be a person trying to ride two horses going in opposite directions at once. Something will have to give: your meditation, your lifestyle, or your sanity.

A student reported as follows:

Saturday

This morning I meditated at the same time, only I stopped a little under the full 20 minutes. My practice...today was not as successful as it could have been for several reasons. One was that I had on semi-tight jeans which hindered me from sitting very comfortably or properly. Secondly, I was rushed to keep an appointment and although

I told myself not to rush it but to take my time, I found myself thinking about it from time to time.

I also experienced quite a bit of monkey mind today—much more than yesterday. My spatial awareness was not the usual awareness of being deep; rather, when I came out of meditation, I had no feeling of coming up from anywhere.

I spent the afternoon at a conference at which I usually fall asleep, and I remained attentive throughout the entire day. I do not really feel that I changed in relation to people except that I felt very "easy-going" in my overall attitude.

Sunday

This morning my meditation could probably be labeled somewhere near disastrous. First, I was not in my apartment but at a friend's house after a very long night of partying and I was not in a healthy physical or mental state...

My entire day started off wrong and continued that way. I felt under the weather and listless for quite some time. Although I do

not blame this for the unsuccessfulness of my
meditation, I am sure that it added to it in
some way.

The conference may have been important,
and only a bluestocking would begrudge a
college student an occasional party night,
whatever the consequences the next morning. But we do get an impression that here is
a life being lived at too fast a clip. There
are too many pulls and pressures and, on
the other side, too many indulgences, for
optimal meditation. The chaos of a lifestyle
that seems always to leave the person about
to miss appointments, about to fall asleep
during meetings, and then partying beyond
reasonable limits in apparent compensation
for those pressures, clearly spills over into
meditation and weakens it.

Even though the student reported positive
effects of meditation, both in keeping awake
and in general in helping her to see what her
lifestyle is doing to her (for the quality of
meditation is a marvelous mirror of one's

whole life), it is evident that the meditation would be improved by a more moderate, better-paced life, as well as the life being improved by regular meditation.

Here is what you need to do with your thoughts, feelings and lifestyle for the great adventure of inward meditative life. Following the advice of the classic teachers of meditation—the Buddha in his Eightfold Path, Patanjali in the Yoga Sutras, and many others—set your mind, your feelings, and your life in order.

First, your mind. Here I would suggest that you sit down and assess as fully and deeply as you can what it is that you accept about spiritual things, the meaning of life, and yourself. As you begin regular meditation, try to make these beliefs a real lodestone, a point of reference, in an often apparently unspiritual and meaningless world.

Endeavor to make all your other thoughts—and actions as well—consistent with these beliefs. Don't believe more than you honestly can. Whether a belief is honest is more important for good meditation than whether it is right or wrong by some external authority. When you find the point of honest belief, align yourself to it. Don't be one person religiously and another at school or home or work, one person in meditation and another at the supermarket or the factory. Anything that compartmentalizes life is bad preparation for meditation.

Second, your feelings and emotions. Here you will best "get it together" for profitable meditation if you are a submarine instead of a speedboat. That is, avoid or rein in frothy surface emotion, so far as is possible without the kind of strained repression of feeling that will leave a depth-charge in your psyche. Keep a lid on impulsive anger, fearful anxiety, and uncontrolled giddiness.

Instead, always remember there is a level of deep, quiet joy beneath the surface. Dive down to it and stay there, which is the real point of meditation. Counteract the surface emotions by trying to see them and the problems that created them clearly and then deal with them responsibly. All this is hard, of course, but it's the only way to go.

Third, your lifestyle. Here the key word is moderation. While there are levels of spirituality that go far beyond any bland moderation-in-all-things approach to life, moderation is a good place to begin. It is far better than running off to excessive indulgence or ill-considered asceticism.

Don't live to eat, but remember health is important to meditation (as well as to almost everything else) and nutrition is important to health; eat sensibly. Live in simplicity without slumming. If you give in to cravings for luxury you'll never have enough and covetous dreams will dog your meditation. So will the grim worries ensconced in real poverty if that is your lot.

Instead, earn an honest living and live within your earnings. Save, spend wisely, give to what is worthy. The great spiritual traditions tell us that worthwhile work, including labor with one's hands, consorts well with good prayer and meditation. So also plain but nourishing food and a solid, well-built but unfancy home and furnishings (whether house, apartment, or mobile home), at a quiet but unpretentious address, agree well with a good meditation life.

As you begin to get these things sorted out, start really meditating. But even if you don't revolutionize your lifestyle overnight, you need not wait before beginning to meditate in earnest. Meditation will help you in the process of regulating your lifestyle, too.

3

Settling Down

I'm ready to start meditating. What do I do?

First you decide when and where. These are important decisions which demand proper attention.

How Long?

The when will depend on how long you plan to meditate. This too is a decision to be made carefully, for there are two possible

44

mistakes regarding length which can set you back. Beginners often make these mistakes.

You may say you'll meditate just as long as you feel like it. This may sound liberal and attractive in our age of reaction against anything that seems "set" and formal. But in meditation it's a no-win program. The feel-like-it approach puts you in thrall to the very subjectivity, the moods and feelings, which you are meditating to transcend. Meditation is, among other things, an effort at disciplining the mind, and you need a set time to make effort and discipline real.

The second mistake: don't make the time too long either. If you set your goal too high, you're likely to be unable to sustain it. You'll get bored, restless, discouraged, and finally give up. Fifteen or twenty minutes is about right for beginners. Pick something in this time range and decide you're going to stick with it for a while.

But you need not be a compulsive clock watcher or get rigid and legalistic about the time. It's no big sin if you're off time once in a while. If a meditation is going very well and you want to keep it up after the time is over, go ahead. If on a particular day you're just absolutely, honestly out of sorts for meditation, and you try it and it's like forcing yourself to eat when you're nauseated, cut it short and then try to figure out what was wrong. To keep away from the distraction of having to look at the clock all the time, set an alarm or timer to go off at the end of the period, or phase the meditation in with a striking clock—start, say, fifteen minutes before the hour and stop when it strikes. Better than an alarm is the inner clock. If you just tell yourself at the beginning of meditation how long you want to go on, the unconscious will let you know when the time's up. Some find this inner clock is very reliable.

Choose a time for meditation when you will have fifteen or twenty minutes free from interruption everyday, and when you are most ready for it in terms of your personal cycle. This will vary with different people.

For some early morning, perhaps before the rest of the house gets up, is best. It is a quiet, free time and meditation is a marvelous way to start the day. But if you're the kind of person who, like me, instinctively grabs every last minute of sleep, really can't wake up until after three cups of coffee, and is always running a few minutes late getting around in the morning, be honest with yourself and try some other time. The human race is divided between larks who function best in the morning and owls who don't really come to life till evening. If you're an owl, find a time in later afternoon or evening when you're at your prime. Don't make it so late you're half asleep, though.

If your work allows, you may find that the best time is during the noon hour, provided you can get free time and privacy.

It is fairly important to meditate at about the same time everyday. This is part of the mild discipline good meditation requires, and enables you to get into a well-grooved pattern by which the benign effects of meditation will best spread into your whole life. But again, be consistent about this without being a fanatic. If things happen that require changing the time on a given day, that's o.k. The lifestyle that good meditation ought to induce is one that is flexible yet persistent, like water finding its way downhill around stumps and boulders, or like a young sapling that can be bent nearly to the ground, yet spring back upright. If you're ice or dead wood, inside you're already fit for the mortician.

WHERE?

Place is important, too. Just as you should meditate at about the same time regularly, so should you meditate in the same place regularly. This is also part of the psychology of establishing a habit and a life-pattern. You build up associations with the place that help you get into the meditation spirit.

Ideally, it should be a corner or some place that is not used for anything else. If you want, you can put there pictures, art objects, flower arrangements and the like, religious or not, according to your own taste as to what goes with meditation. I don't mean by this that you should make your own shrine or chapel. To me at least, that would be too much fuss. (But if you really want to, why not?) In fact, if the whole idea of a special place sounds like too much fuss, you may prefer just to meditate in the middle of the living room or on your bed.

The important thing is a regular place that is quiet, clean, and private. If you live in a cabin in the woods miles from civilization, that's wonderful, but even if you live next door to a freeway or a boiler plant, find the quietest place—at least the place that is most free of household noise on top of the steady drone of traffic or factory. Steady noise is not so bad; the worst thing is sharp irregular noise like kitchen clatter or voices from people or TV that make you want to half-listen.

The place should be reasonably clean and free of clutter. A cluttered place subtly but inevitably reflects and creates a cluttered mind, which is unable to concentrate and get down to basic simplicities. Best is a room that is simply furnished and with everything in its place. (Here again, though, be consistent and persistent without being fanatic. One stray sock on the floor is not going to ruin a whole meditation.)

Obviously, it should also be private. Nothing is more distastrous for meditation than someone else who is not meditating futzing around in the room. Of course, if you are meditating *with* someone else, or a group, with whom you feel good, that is entirely different. While not necessary, other meditators can powerfully strengthen meditation.

WHAT POSTURE?

Time and place squared away, let's proceed. One more matter that has to be settled is the posture you will take. The usual Eastern position is seated on the floor or earth cross-legged. Some religious Westerners, because of the associations of meditation with prayer, have meditated kneeling, at a prayer desk or against a chair or bed. Other people have found that meditating seated in a chair works best for them. The only essential is that the position be free of pain and strain, yet not so relaxed as to promote lethargy; that it be a stable posture you can maintain without wiggling for the alloted period; and that it have the right associations for you.

If you sit cross-legged on the floor, the ideal, though hard to achieve, is the so-called lotus posture, with each shoeless foot resting on the thigh of the other leg, soles up. This position has to the highest degree what is the asset of the cross-legged posture: stability and a low center of gravity. It makes you feel like you're rooted in the earth and if you were pushed over, you'd pop back up. The two knees should be touching the floor, making with your bottom a triangle, the strongest form there is.

You may be able to learn to stretch out your thighs by degrees, but don't force or strain. You can injure yourself. To keep the knees down to the floor, sit on a small cushion. It should be hard and firm, not a bed pillow. Don't sit in the middle of it, but on the edge, just enough to raise you so that the knees are down to ground level or at least near enough so that you can slowly train them down. If you want to go all out, the stylish thing would be to get one of the small round black pill-shaped cushions used by Zen monks, which can be purchased at various Zen centers and specialty shops. But grandma's sofa cushion or a folded-up blanket will work just as well.

If you can't manage a full lotus, which you probably can't unless you are extraordinarily young and supple, or an acrobat or gymnast in top shape, try a half-lotus (one foot up) or quarter-lotus (one foot up inside the knee rather than the thigh). Or just sit in the so-called Burmese posture, with the legs crossed and knees on the floor, but the shins simply resting parallel to each other, each foot touching the calf of the other leg. If none of this feels right, sit tailor-style, knees up. As with so much else, posture is something to test and persevere in, not something to be fanatic about.

If you sit in a chair, use one that is not bone-wracking but firm enough to keep you alert. Davenports and easy chairs are to read and snooze in, not meditate. A straight chair with a padded seat and no arms, like a dining-table chair, would be about right. Sit with your legs and feet parallel, feet resting flat on the floor (not crossed!).

Whether you sit on the floor, kneel, or sit in a chair, the remaining details of good posture are about the same. Keep the back upright. It doesn't have to be ramrod straight like a soldier on parade. You don't want any strain. But on the other hand, slouchy posture will definitely produce a slouchy mind. If you are on the floor, there is nothing wrong with supporting your back with a wall or bedrest if you want, so long as you support it straight. If you kneel, keep both knees parallel on the floor and kneel upright against your support, your body from knees to crown at a ninety degree angle to the floor.

What do you do with your hands? Much has been made of how you hold your hands in various schools of meditation. Symbolic meaning is attached to some of them, such as the "full moon," an emblem of Nirvana, made by Zen meditators by laying the left hand on the right, palms upward, and raising the thumbs and pressing their tips together to make a circle. The Christian prayer gesture, palms pressed together, suggests an attitude of supplication.

If a gesture like this is meaningful to you, do it. But for meditation as such the only important thing is that the hands be kept quiet and out of the way. Meditation is not handwork. They can be folded and laid in the lap, or rested on the knees. Don't put them behind the head or anything like that.

The head should be held erect or slightly tilted forward. The mouth should be closed.

The eyes can be open or closed. Some people can hardly meditate without the eyes shut (lightly shut, not squeezed tight). Others find that this induces sleepiness, dreaminess, wandering fantasies, retinal images, and such hindrances to good meditation. They prefer to keep the eyes open, or better about half open, and concentrate on some steadying focus, such as a candle, object, picture or even just a blank wall or, if you prefer to tilt the head forward slightly, a blank piece of floor some four feet in front of you. These possible visual focuses will be discussed more fully later.

STARTING

Now that you're set, what do you do next?

Some people like to light a stick or pinch of incense, finding that the pleasant aroma with its religious overtones is conducive to meditation. If so it seems to you, do it; if incense feels too fussy and alien, don't.

Next start breathing slowly and deeply, from the abdomen. Breath is important to good meditation. Regular breathing has a calming effect; deep breathing increases oxidation and makes you quietly zestful and alert. As in all things, use moderation in breathing control; don't breathe so deeply as to bring about strain, or so regularly that it becomes hypnotic, like a metronome.

Now, what do you do with your mind? Remember again that the purpose of meditation is really not to think of things, however beautiful and inspirational, but to rest and refresh the mind by allowing it to return to its natural state. It is the Quiet Mind. What you will do with it, then, is things which gently but firmly impede its Monkey, Sloth, and Cow systems of activity. You will not give it more to do, but less and less, until it has geared way down and found a Tranquillity Base. There are several methods to attain this end. Here a few very simple and basic ones will be suggested. What we want is really the simplest possible path to) the Center.

COUNTING BREATHS

The first method is counting breaths. Count your breaths—1 on the inhalation, 2 on the exhalation and so forth—silently from 1 to 10, then start all over again. This may seem like an absurd thing to do, but you may be surprised at how nicely it shakes the mind down until other levels of consciousness can seep through. On the other hand, for a while it will probably also teach you how little control you really have of your mind. You will lose count, forget about counting while the Monkey Mind races all over the place in glee, and find even the amount of concentration that such a simple thing as counting breaths requires is both stressful and boring. Keep at it; the rewards will be worth it. If you lose count or your mind wanders, don't worry about it. Don't feel guilty, discouraged, or upset. It's o.k. Just go back to 1 again and start all over. Try to get so you can count breaths from 1 to 10 for ten minutes without missing any or going past 10. The help this will give your ability to concentrate, both in meditation and outside, may well be measurable.

A couple of variations. Count only the inhalations. Count backwards, like a spaceflight countdown, from 10 to 1. This has not only the connotation of preparing to blast off in your inner exploration, but also the interesting metaphysical connotation of suggesting the return from multiplicity to the One.

Here is another technique. I would suggest you first master breath counting, then go on to the new technique with the aid of your enhanced ability to concentrate. It is simply mindfulness of breathing. Instead of counting breaths, just follow your breaths with your mind, in and out, in and out. Try this for several minutes. Just let your breaths be the quiet, relaxed focus of your attention.

The real purpose of all of this is to produce what is sometimes called one-pointed concentration. Our usual problem is that the mind is not resting on one thing. We are leaping wildly about with the Monkey, climbing aimlessly around with the Sloth, or chewing the cud with the Cow. The first thing to do in meditation, then, is to bring the mind to rest by focusing on one thing that will stop that pointless activity. It should be something as simple, close to hand, and void of further suggestive meaning as breathing; we don't want a focus of one-pointed concentration that will shoot off a fresh Roman candle of busy thought.

However, there are other focuses besides breaths. One is posture. Particularly if you are able to achieve a good solid pose like the full lotus, simply be aware of it. Without active thought, simply be conscious of your stability, your rootedness on the earth, your calm beneath the sky. Be a still point at the center of the universe. (If the universe is infinite, all places are equally its center.) Feel the posture and that's all; know your calm and superb physical-mental being.

Other possibilities include visual, auditory, and mental points of concentration. Most of these will be discussed in the next chapter. Especially when breaths become so tedious you feel that, for all its ultimate value, you've just got to shift for a time to something different and with a little more meat in it, the use of a mantra or short chant can be useful for beginners.

MANTRAS

The mantra is said silently, just in the mind or at most with the mouth moving slightly. Again, the idea is not to think *about* it. Just let it be. Just keep it moving in the mind as a quiet, nonintense focus of mental attention.

For this reason the mantra *can* be a syllable or phrase that is perfectly meaningless to you, just one whose sound you like. "Ba...Ba...Ba..." or "Hrim... Hrim...Hrim..." or "Vrundalore...Vrundalore...Vrundalore..." In this case it functions about like counting breaths, or mindfulness of breathing.

However, it can also be a word or phrase whose meaning has good, appropriate associations for you. This usage contains the danger that you are going to start, even against your will, to thinking *about* that meaning. But if you can keep the discursive mind on short leash, you may find that the meaning does slip unobtrusively into your meditation and your life to deepen it without your having to think about it; that is ideal.

Here are some possibilities. My wife, a Quaker like myself, likes to use the phrase, "Let thy Light shine through me." It is reminiscent of the Quaker emphases on the Inner Light and that there is "that of God in every one." It also lets seep into the meditator the realization that meditation is not to be for oneself only, but to make one a lens through which light can shine into a dark world.

You can simply repeat the word *One*: "One...One...One..." In a sense that says it all. One God, one universe, one undivided self, all beings united in love.

I like a line from the Upanishads of ancient India: "Only in the Infinite is there joy," perhaps shortened to "Infinite Joy." It reminds us that there is no lasting satisfaction in anything less than the unlimited primal reality we begin to tap in meditation, for all else is changing and passing away.

One that has been very common in the Christian tradition, especially in Eastern Christianity, is the so-called Jesus prayer, the heart of that great classic of Russian spirituality, *The Way of a Pilgrim*. In its full form it is, "Lord Jesus Christ, Son of God, have mercy upon me." It can he shortened to the Greek *Christe eleison* of the Liturgy, that is, "Christ have mercy," or even to simply repeating the name "Jesus...Jesus...

Jesus..." over and over, as St. Francis of Assisi was wont to do in prayer/meditation.

Other Christians like to use the Doxology, "Glory be to the Father, the Son, and the Holy Spirit..." or phrases like "God's love" or "Praise the Lord!"

Some people like to use a chant in a foreign language, especially an ancient sacred tongue, which has meaning but not a superficial English meaning. There is no shortage of these: the Sanskrit *Om Mani Padme Hum*, "Om the Jewel in the Lotus Hum," representing the union of the Absolute and the phenomenal world; the Arabic *Allah Akbar* (God is Great), the Greek *Christe eleison* already mentioned; and monosyllables like the Sanskrit *Om* which represents Brahman, absolute reality itself, and its Sino-Japanese reverse *Mu* which represents Emptiness, the Buddhist Void which is also all things.

Some spiritual traditions, mainly Eastern, stress that a mantra can be given to a student only by a guru or teacher who has deep insight into the student's temperament and will assign one suitable to the person. They also stress that mantras have meaning as words of power in themselves, the sounds being aligned to lines of spiritual force in the cosmos, so you should use only one that possesses such esoteric potency that it will work for good whether you understand its meaning or not. Sanskrit mantras, for example, are like this. There is undoubtedly some level of truth to all this, and there is nothing wrong with using a traditional Sanskrit mantra and even receiving one from a guru.

However, our purpose is to present meditation without mystification for Westerners to whom ideas like this may be too alien to be helpful. Use any mantra you want, then. Devise your own, tailor-made to your individual nature. We assume that a mantra can work very well just by the meaning you give it and the associations it has for you.

Say the mantra slowly and steadily, not reflectively, but in a soft easy rhythm. As it works into your mind and heart, its effect will be felt and benign changes of consciousness will come. Some people, whether or not of Catholic background, have found that saying the mantra on a rosary or chain of beads helps, one repetition to each bead.

You are likely to find that your mantra will not stop when formal meditation does, but may keep on going as you turn to other things. You may find it working in your mind at other times of the day, too, as you work or play. So long as it does not become obsessive, that is all right too. It is a way in which the benefits of meditation can be conveyed to the rest of your life; when the mantra is going, something of the meditation's peace and power are not far behind.

Even at the very beginning of meditation as a practice in your life, when you get time, place, method, and posture together, you can get significant results that encourage you. You can feel calmed, refreshed, and even enjoy rewarding experiences of joy and meaning.

Here is a student's account of an initial meditation.

Day 1

My first day of meditation. I began at 6:15 and ended at 6:35 a.m. I used the counting breaths technique in a quarter lotus position. Legs just wouldn't go any higher. Only had about 5 hours of sleep last night, but I feel quite refreshed right now. I had a little trouble at first keeping thoughts out of my head but when I intensified the numbers in my head and made them a part of my breath, I was able to focus on them much better.... Everything was so quiet and all I could hear was my rhythmic deep breathing. An intense feeling would come and go often, one I don't normally experience—perhaps a rush of energy.... I think I was just getting warmed up.

Start then, and keep on going.

4

Advanced Settling Down

You're all set. The lights are low, you're seated comfortably on a cushion in, we'll say, a quarter lotus. A whiff of incense is in the air. You "center down" mentally and begin slow, deep breathing, counting the breaths from one to ten.

You then practice simple "mindfulness of breathing" for a time, just feeling your life, your existence, your being itself. You are part of the universe of air, light, stars, and vital energy. Your mind is the reflexive side of this existence, Being knowing itself. You may pass into a mantra, saying "Life... energy," Life...energy," over and over to the rhythm of your breathing, till all is stilled save sheer abstract life and energy themselves.

This time, though, you feel ready for something more than breath-counting, mindfulness of breathing, and mantra. You need another anchor for the mind, one that opens up another aspect of meditative consciousness. Here are some possibilities.

VISUAL FOCUSES

One of the most common devices for "one-pointed" meditation to stop the action is focusing the gaze on a candle. The glowing soft-bright point of a candle flame provides an ideal spot for visual concentration, which in turn stops the action of the mind. Let your eyes just gaze at it steadily and gently. Don't look at it with an intense, squinting stare; on the other hand, don't let your eyes move away from the flame during the time of meditation except for normal blinks. Avoid strain and distraction. While you focus on the candle flame you can continue mindfulness of breathing or mantra chanting, or you can just appreciate the Quiet Mind induced by the candle, allowing it to grow deeper and more joyful in its own way.

You don't have to use a candle for visual concentration. Anything that focuses the gaze can do it; a corner of the room, a spot on the wall, the top of a bedpost. In the Theravada Buddhist tradition, small discs in various colors are used. As is well known, different colors have different psychological impacts, and the choice can have a very subtle, unobtrusive influence on the mood into which you gradually move as you meditate. If you have been riled up and need to cool off and calm down, try blue or green. If you need to energize yourself, try orange or red. If you have been in the dumps and want to lift yourself into a happy or exalted state of consciousness, use lavender, gold, or silver-white. Just look at the disc and count breaths, being mindful of breathing or saying a mantra.

May pictures, statues, or symbols such as a cross or a star be used as visual focuses for meditation? This is a question which requires discussion. The short answer is yes, of course they may be—but for two reasons careful attention needs to be given to the choice of symbols.

First, the danger is always present that the content of the object will give rise to reflective thought that, however good in itself, will militate against the purpose of meditation as leading one into the Quiet Mind.

Second, the content of the object is likely, if only subliminally, to shape the mood and philosophical interpretation of the meditation. So far we have been talking about general meditation. But once you introduce a painting of mountains and streams, or a crucifix, or the Sanskrit symbol for *Om*, you are bound to get (in capital letters) Nature Mysticism, Christian Meditation, or Hindu Meditation. The mood and meaning of meditation is bound to such obvious symbols, and they dictate special interpretations of the experience. Your gaze will bounce off the picture, image, or symbol and come back packaged; instead of being a freeform exploration of yourself in the Quiet Mind state, your meditation will be an exercise in enhancing inwardly your growth in a tradition to which you have made a prior commitment. There is nothing wrong with that if you have made a deliberate, thoughtful decision to be a Nature Mystic, a Christian or a Hindu. But be aware of the tremendous subliminal power of symbols; don't use them unless you know what you're doing.

If you feel good about your religious tradition and it's important to you that it be integrated into your meditation life, then by all means introduce a symbol from it as a focus for visual meditation. Use a cross or crucifix, a picture of Jesus or one of the saints, a Buddha seated in meditation, an *Om* or Hindu deity. If your orientation is more toward the wonder—if you wish, the divine—packed into the world of nature or the marvels unveiled by modern science, choose a nature picture that well expresses your feeling for it, or a picture of Saturn or distant galaxies. If symbols have meaning for you but you prefer they be nonsectarian, take a general symbol of aspiration or transcendence, such as a stylized star, sun, or bird in flight. If you are any good at arts or crafts, paint or make your own picture, image, or symbol; its style will be more personal and so will its "vibes."

If, however, at this point you are content just to practice pure meditation for the sake of the simple mental refreshment it affords, or to see where it leads on its own, then hold off on heavily charged symbols or pictures. Use the breathing methods, a relatively neutral mantra, or focus visually on a candle or a corner of the room or a circle of color. Later, after your practice has stabilized, bring in other things if you wish. Remember that you don't *have* to have a lot of holy paraphernalia around to be devout, though it's fine if you like it. Zen monks meditate facing a bare wall, and the Christian St. Anthony meditated in a desert cave. In all spiritual traditions many of the most saintly souls dispense with most external objects of piety in order to find God everywhere. Do whatever seems most natural and unstrained. The important thing is a good meditation.

SOUNDS

What about an auditory focus, the use of sound, for one-pointed meditation? In my experience and in that of others I know about, artificial sounds are not good, but steady, regular natural sounds can be extremely beneficial. One would be hard put to explain exactly why this is, for the same distinction does not obtain for visual images, though, as we have seen, such manmade devices as pictures and constructed symbols need to be used with some caution.

However, the two obvious artificial possibilities, music and a steady or rhythmic tone, do not work very well in practice. Music may be relaxing and refreshing in its own way, but it does not fit at all with the kind of stopping-the-action, Quiet Mind meditation we have been talking about. Even if it is soft, "meditative" music, the kind of mood it puts one in is a drifting, daydreamy reverie, not true stillness. Play it before and after your meditation, but not during it. A mood is not meditation; the trouble with music is that the melody flows along, carrying you with it, and there is nothing to hold to as a one-pointed focus.

For this reason some have proposed artificial "one-pointed" sounds to focus meditation, such as a soft steady hum or a beep-beep or pong-pong. My feeling is that, first of all, the associations are all wrong: these devices sound like something from a lab or maybe from *Star Trek*. Second, I think the effect is likely to be more hypnotic than truly meditative. There are obvious parallels between hypnosis—especially self-hypnosis—and meditation, but there are also very important differences. Self-hypnosis can be a very benign and useful procedure, but its purpose is a little different. It is usually intended to alter behavior by putting you into a half-sleep state of consciousness in which your usual barriers are down and you are open to suggestion. Meditation is stopping the action while remaining highly alert and open, not to suggestion, but to experience, experience of the reality of self and world. Steady mechanical humming or beeps or pongs would, I think, tend to induce a semisleep state and get in the way of clear meditative experience.

On the other hand, there is nothing better than steady pounding rain on the roof or the regular chirping of crickets and cicadas. Just as good is the chirp of morning birds and the sigh of a soft wind in trees, especially pines.

If you can open your ears to sounds like this as a focus, you will be blessed. Don't listen *to* the sound; just keep on it as a pilot keeps on the beam, and follow through your meditation.

Perhaps there is a subjective reason why steady natural sounds are better. Meditation is intended to lift us out of the ordinary gamut of human experience and contrivance. We instinctively sense that nature is something larger than the human, something that is one step further along toward the Infinite. In seeking recourse in nature we are lifted up and out, as well as in; in the meditation situation, the human alone does not go so far. So if you wish an auditory focus, let nature provide it.

THE KOAN

Human language can perhaps take us farther, if only because of its paradoxical quality. Language can make us face the limits as well as the potentials of the human mind, and confronting those limits can incite powerful meditative break-throughs. Nowhere is this better illustrated than in the use of the koan.

The koans (pronounced koh-ans) are the enigmatic riddles or puzzle-words used by some Zen students as a focus for meditation. They serve at the same time to lead the mind to experience itself in a fresh way. Examples are "What is the sound of one hand?" or "What was your face before you were born?"

Both of these have a deep meaning in Buddhist philosophy. The sound of one hand is the pregnant silence of the universe itself prior to its breakdown, through our half-blinded perception, into the noise of "two hands"—the confusion of many things seen as separate rather than as part of that unimaginable unity. The face you had before you were born is the ultimate true nature you have now, have always had, and always will have, an eternal Buddhahood.

But the purpose of koans is not to lead you to think these things out intellectually, but to let their marvelous paradoxes sink in, deeper, deeper, and deeper. Just hold the koan in your mind without thinking *about* it, just saying it over and over and over, like a mantra. "What is the sound of one hand?...What is the sound of one hand? ...What is the sound of one hand?..." The riddle will serve as a one-pointed focus, at the same time goading you subliminally into ineffable inner experience along the lines of its meaning.

You can use a traditional Zen koan if you wish. Here are some, slightly modified in some cases to make them intelligible without the whole anecdote in which they were embedded:

"When a flag is flapping in the wind, what moves?" The Mind.

"What is the Buddha? Three pounds of flax." Said by a monk who apparently was asked this question while busy weighing out the flax harvest.

"What is the Buddha? The hedge at the back of the garden."

"When you finish eating, wash the dishes."

"In the trees fish play, in the deep sea birds are flying." Remember our earlier reference to flying fish and diving birds as they relate to meditation experience.

"Why did Bodhidharma come from the West?" According to tradition, Bodhidharma was the monk who brought Zen from India to China.

"How can meditation make a Buddha?"

"Who is the teacher?"

"What is the ultimate teaching?"

"Be quiet."

Remember, *don't answer the koan*, even those that are in the form of questions. Just keep asking the question. You will be surprised what a strange and rich effect that will have.

A very good koan for asking but not answering is one which has been used by some modern Zen masters, as well as a question put by countless humans of all times. It is simply, "Who am I?" Make this inquiry of yourself over and over without bothering with an intellectual answer. You will find it working itself into the depths of your consciousness, peeling away one plausible answer after another by showing that behind each answer lies another deeper question, or rather another putting of the same endless question, "Who am I?" (Because it is endless, this is a powerful but scary koan. Don't use it unless you are absolutely sure you can handle it. It's a strong persistent fellow who is likely to stay with you even after you get up from meditation, and to keep coming back even after you tell him to go away for awhile. And as you go deeper and deeper with subliminal answers that won't hold still and the question comes through louder and louder, it can become terrifying and make you think you're going crazy, until you've worked it through and know how to live with it. Then its tremendous strength becomes yours. But be careful—not everyone succeeds in mastering this one.)

As a modern meditator, you can devise your own koans. Fit them to what you do. "How does a Buddha mow the grass?" "Or cook supper?" "Or sell hardware or stocks?"

When it's cloudy: "Where did the sky go?" When it's sunny: "Where did the clouds go?"

When you're down, say, possessed by a love that seems unreturned: "*Who* is in love? *Who* is loved?" Fit it in with "Who am I?" and watch the bad feelings dissipate and go where the clouds went when the sky was clear.

An acquaintance of mine who had been very close to his grandmother as a child, after her death used the koan, "Where's Grandma?" He had said this innumerable times as a boy—now the query had new, unanswerable significance.

When you're happy, say "The balloon goes up," and in your mind's eye watch a balloon ascend higher and higher until it disappears, leaving only empty and marvelous joy.

Always bear in mind, though, that koan work is difficult and to be done with care. I would not recommend that anyone begin meditation with it. As I have suggested, start with breaths, then go on to a fairly neutral mantra, and then let a koan take the place of the mantra if you wish.

The problem is twofold. First, you need to have some experience with meditation and know for yourself what a meditation state of mind is really like, know from simple examples what a "one-pointed" focus is and does. Otherwise you are overwhelmingly likely to intellectualize about the koan instead of using it as it is meant to be used, as a focus which works into your consciousness only subliminally. But intellectualizing will defeat the whole purpose of meditation, and of the koan.

Second and more serious, koans do have real power. For a beginner on his or her own, it can be like a kid with his first license trying to drive a semi. The koan can dig deep and, depending on the person and which koan it is, tear the scar tissue off old psychic wounds and open doors to nameless fears locked in since childhood, or let out strange fantasies and visions. You need stability and experience to deal with all this. The process of mastering a koan, so that its strength becomes yours, can be like going through a sort of temporary insanity, for its irrationality, its unanswerable question, seems to knock away all the supports for our working notions that this is a rational universe which can be handled in reasonable ways.

For these reasons, spiritual tradition has insisted that koans, like mantras, should only be assigned by a master to a disciple, and used under his or her guidance. In Zen this means that the master will periodically have an interview with the student and ask his charge what his koan is and what it means. He will look for demonstrations that the postulant has truly interiorized its inexpressible meaning, so that he or she has not just "head" knowledge of it, but that its force permeates the deepest strands of life and so comes out in fresh, spontaneous and uncalculated ways. For example, in response to the koan "What is the sound of one hand?" the student might say nothing, but just thrust one hand forward with instant lightning-like vigor behind which the whole self—mind, feelings, and body—is united in a single gesture, perhaps even powerfully striking the master with the force of the gesture. In the same way, the master can tell if a koan is *not* working for a particular person and recommend a change.

If you want to do koan work with a Zen master, fine. There are some two dozen Zen centers in the United States, Britain, and the Commonwealth where it can be done in English. However, this book is written primarily for people who cannot, or do not wish to, work with an external teacher. Its presupposition is that if you are reasonably intelligent and in good mental health, there is nothing wrong with doing meditation on your own. It may in fact be for the best.

TEACHERS OR NOT?

Spiritual mentors can be helpful if understanding and well qualified, as some are. But they are also fallible, and pages could be written about mistakes certain ones have made in dealing with various individuals. Further, there is the danger that if one becomes too attached to a wise fatherly or motherly teacher, a dependency relationship will be set up that actually inhibits spiritual growth. Meditation ought to help you grow in inner freedom and in taking charge of your own life, not be a means by which you become the child of another. Perhaps the best thing that a spiritual master can do is simply show that one can advance far beyond where most of us are, and thereby inspire us to become masters ourselves.

In so doing you can, I am convinced, be your own teacher—or better, let that within which is your highest potential for growth be your teacher in actualizing itself. With the informal help of books and like-minded friends, you can develop the program for meditation and inner life that is right for you. If you believe in yourself and open yourself to your own best and most honest insights about yourself, you can ascertain far better than anyone else what regimen, what visual focus, or what koans will work best for your case. You may make mistakes, but then so can highly touted teachers. Just keep tab on how things are going, and if something seems to be seriously wrong —that is, if you find that you are unable to concentrate, or that depression, anxiety, or fears and unwholesome fantasies are only increasing—immediately stop, reassess your program, and seek psychological help if the problem is severe and does not go away.

If you are basically the secure, commonsensical person for whom this book is

intended, though, you should find the
benefits of meditation much outweigh any
problems and that you can very satisfactor-
ily be your own scout in the galaxies of
meditation. This will, in fact, be a highly
satisfying and valuable task. As you plan
your meditation life by analyzing yourself
and your needs, you will learn much that is
good to know about yourself that might not
have surfaced otherwise. You will grow in
self-awareness as you grow in meditation's
poise and power.

As the poet Tennyson said:

> Self-reverence, self-knowledge,
> self-control,
> These three alone lead life to
> sovereign power.

5

When You Get There, Keep On Going

Suppose you have underway a good program of meditation based on breath-
counting or even beginning koans. You
know what the Quiet Mind is and how to
reach it. It's great. But you feel that even
though you're this far, there must be some
way you can keep on going, some way
meditation can be deepened and enriched.
This is a good feeling. Anything can be improved. There is always another mountain
range to be crossed.

In the case of meditation, though, it needs to be balanced against another consideration. One should not get too hung up on "making headway" in the art. Any meditation that helps you to quiet the mind and experience something of your true reality, that counteracts the Monkey, Sloth, and Cow Minds, is a good meditation. Concern for "progress" can easily become an obsession which gets in the way of the immense good that simple, unprepossessing, but sincere meditation can do. You don't *have* to try every technique and explore every nook and cranny of meditation's universe. What seems more advanced in yourself or others can actually be less advanced, by most any criteria of the spiritual life, if it means more preoccupation with your own ego and state of spiritual health, a devastating temptation which has ruined many a potential meditator, not to mention many a potential saint or buddha. Don't always be taking your inner temperature or worrying about cloud fronts in the mind. Just meditate calmly, peacefully, for the good it does and the power it brings. If things go wrong in some particular meditation, instead of agonizing over them or thinking you've *got* to try something new, just brush them aside and keep on.

But if you can avoid the precipice of egocentric agonizing, keep off the scowling cliffs of inflexibility on the other side as well. As we have observed already, the meditator's personality ought to be fresh and supple, like the young sapling full of life that bends with the breeze and then springs back, not like dead wood. In this lively, playful spirit, then, vary your meditation methods and try to deepen, enrich, and expand your meditation life.

First, you can lengthen the time, say to half an hour. This will take a little bit of stretching at first. It will mean more time alotted to preliminary breath-counting, then to silent mindfulness of breathing, then to the mantra or koan if you are using one.

After that, you may now find yourself led to devote some remaining meditation time to just letting the meditation go where it will. This is something only a fairly experienced meditator should do since, at the beginning stages, it can seem like just a license for thinking gorgeous thoughts or even just woolgathering, which as we have seen involves serious misunderstandings of what meditation is about. Now, try to keep a delicate balance between giving yourself freedom to see where the meditation wants to go and indulging in mere fantasy and daydreaming.

Thus, if you find yourself irresistibly drawn to thinking about a particular person or situation, that may not be just a wandering-mind situation. It may now mean that you *ought* to meditate for and about that person or situation—or pray for him, her, or it, if you are comfortable with such religious language. Think calmly and lovingly, holding the person or situation gently in the light. (We will talk more later about meditating for others.)

You may find yourself drawn to think about, or better yet, just to be aware of God or Ultimate Reality. Follow your lead; this is what is known in some traditions as the contemplative prayer into which meditation can flow, and when it does the lower level of spirituality should be suspended and give way to the higher. It would be presumptuous here to say too much about this high and subtle state, since it is a very individual thing and in any case one must assume that now God or Ultimate Reality itself is taking over, and one can only go where it leads. Remember, though, that meditation is an experience state, not a thinking-out state. Just endeavor to *know* God or Ultimate Reality, not to try to figure out what you are touching in theological, philosophical, or scientific language. To do so would immediately cut you off from the direct experience and throw you back onto a figuring-out level of mind. Save that for later.

Another thing that may happen when you let meditation take you where it will is that thoughts and ideas seem to pop into the mind when it is Quiet. Often these will be valuable insights, not only to practical problems you may have, but also to philosophical or religious difficulties that are bothering you. This is what some spiritual authorities call the prayer of listening, listening for the voice of God.

One may hold that these insights come from God, from a Guardian Angel, or from one's own unconscious when its wisdom is allowed to rise up by stilling the turbulence of the superficial mind. These meditation insights should not be considered beyond question, as though they were some infallible oracle; certain of them may be notions from dubious corners of the mind that have somehow wandered into the mainstream of consciousness, or, in religious language, may be Satan disguised as an angel of light. But often exceedingly valuable ideas do appear, as though from nowhere, in the last and deepest stage of meditation.

How does one tell whether what appears when meditation is allowed to go its own way is meditation for another, contemplation, listening, or whether it is mere fantasy? The best way is to discern whether it really seems to be a product of the initial stopping-the-action meditation state, or a relapse back to the Monkey Mind state or whatever was there before meditation. Is it really beaming in on a deeper level to which stopping the action opened access? Does the material arise out of deep calm as though it belonged there in the center of the calm, like a lotus growing out of a still lake? If so it is genuine meditation. But if it seems to force its way in and then, picking up steam, carries you off down a garden path of pointless but exciting ideas and fantasies, it is something you need to let go of, if need be by returning to counting breaths or mindfulness of breathing.

You can, then, meditate for half an hour, leaving time for letting the meditation take you where it will. If your schedule allows and you feel genuinely drawn to do so, you can meditate for half an hour morning and evening.

I would not recommend that most ordinary people meditate *more* than a total of an hour a day. Meditation is supposed to be the mainspring of your life, not all your life. You need plenty of "other" life to provide scope to let the peace, warmth, and love streaming out of your meditation affect family and friends, work and the world, for good. Even most monks and nuns, unless in highly contemplative traditions, do not spend much more than an hour a day in formal meditation, and in an ordinary person more than that is likely to become escapist and unbalanced. An hour, or for many people even less, is enough to generate enough power to last through a day; thereafter the important thing is to carry your meditation into other arenas of life, a challenge just as great and just as important as a good meditation itself.

Sometimes the problem is that the other arenas impinge on meditation. At the beginning it is important to shield yourself in meditation as much as possible from extraneous noise and interruption. But as you mature in it, you can learn to use the outside world creatively and deepen your relationship to it. It becomes something to love rather than shun. In the process, you can learn to do "spot" meditations of great value in all sorts of times and places.

Two attitudes to the outside world are possible during meditation—closed and open. The closed, necessary to beginners, is what we have been talking about mostly so far, although we have noted, for example, that the sound of rain or crickets can be an excellent focus of awareness. That, with the potential for attuning you to the infinities of nature, is moving into the open attitude.

But what about the sound of people laughing and talking in the next room, or children playing outside, or of traffic and industry? They can be distracting, to be sure.

Nonetheless, if you can—through breath-counting and mindfulness of breathing, mantras or koans—move into a deep open state of consciousness (like that described above for letting the meditation take you where it will), those sounds can themselves be like the appearance of people you need to meditate for, voices coming to the prayer of listening, or even manifestions of God or Ultimate Reality for your meditation universe. Meditation does not mean, in the last analysis, cutting yourself off from the world, but uniting yourself to it on deep levels, so its life is your life and you are one in love and being with all creatures. But it is no good holding to that unity in theory if you cannot accept it in practice in the form of the specific people and noises within ear-shot.

Let meditation take you to a formless, timeless state before the emergence of the universe. Then let forms appear: a galaxy here, a smiling lovable face there. Let the laughter in the next room, the happy shouts of play, the hum of industry be the appearance of the universe with which you are one; hear its messages, pray for it, see the divine in it. Hold it in consciousness like a koan, the greatest and most mysterious koan of all; hold it but don't try to resolve it. Then as you get up let it go.

Another thing to try, related to this, is deliberately to meditate in unusual places, perhaps places where the peace and love of meditation are much needed: in nature, in offices, in busses, in hospitals, where crime is rife. This is another step which requires some maturity in meditation. But it is very important and an opportunity for immense growth, both for you and others.

These kinds of meditation require flexibility; one cannot always have access to familiar props and postures. They require an attitude which veers very far in the direction of the open rather than the closed approach. They may very well mandate that you forego some of your own peace for the sake of others. But they are worth it.

The easiest meditation of this class, and the one most oriented to personal needs, is meditating in nature. I would not recommend this to absolute beginners. Nature is too rich, too full of distractions of all sorts—from spectacular sunsets to dive-bombing mosquitoes—too liable to pull one into a mere aestheticism to be advisable when one is simply mastering basic techniques and attitudes. For that a room as close to four bare walls as possible is best. But after you feel you have stabilized your practice to a reasonable extent, try some nice day going out and sitting for meditation in the midst of nature. Whether it is a still glade in a national forest, a bench in a city park, a sandy sunlit beach, a cornfield, a creekside, or your own back yard, find some place in the open that is shady, comfortable, beautiful, and free from intrusion as possible. If it is a public place and you don't want to be self-conscious, just meditate sitting in a normal manner rather than cross-legged or in a lotus posture.

Follow the usual procedure, but perhaps for a koan use something like "What is the sky?" or, in summer, "Where has the snow gone?" or, at any time, "All in the flower" or "All in the leaf," for the whole of God or Ultimate Reality or Nature is indivisible and is contained as fully in a single flower or leaf, or a single atom, as in galaxies.

Then, when the time comes for supreme openness and listening, make yourself aware of the nature around you and the messages in it. Open your eyes and *see*, see every flower and leaf and bird and cloud just as it is, without subjective interpretation, but like an artist or poet just seeing it for what it is in itself, in its form and color and vibrancy. You will then see it as it is to itself and to God, full of glory.

Once, meditating in the rich deep forests near the sea in the Big Sur region of California, as usual I went inward with my eyes closed for a while, then opened them and looked around. Right on the first moment of opening I was astounded and humbled by the potent, almost psychedelic splendor of everything. It was the universe as it must really be, charged through and through with the sublimity of Absolute Reality. Only gradually, as I kept looking, did it fade back into the light of common day, magnificent enough in that setting.

Nature mysticism can, however, easily become narcissistic, something enjoyed self-centeredly just for its own sake. Be sure to extend love to all creatures of woodland or back yard. The Tibetan Buddhists have a custom of dedicating the merit of every spiritual exercise to the liberation of all sentient beings by using a definite prayer or act of devotion to this purpose. This is a good practice; emulate it, especially in nature. For nature meditation will lose more than half its real value if it does not make you more loving to all beings—animal or human, in city or country, at all times, whether you feel like it or not.

6

Meditation and Your Life

Regular meditation ought to have a profound interaction with the way the remainder of your life is lived. . . and enjoyed. While it offers no miracle cure, it can help you deal positively with problem situations, negative habits, and the attitudes that lie behind them.

We have already, in Chapter 2, surveyed the lifestyle patterns that are conducive to good meditation. Now it is time to see how, in turn, meditation can affect your lifestyle, particularly when its force is focused on a special aspect. For meditation can impinge on the rest of your life in two ways: first, by setting a general tone which can determine the way *everything* is done; and second, by providing a mighty weapon to aim at trouble spots.

First the general tone. Giving time to the Quiet Mind will bring down the stress level of the whole of your day a few notches, not only for the time immediately after meditation, just as putting an ice cube in a glass of water cools the whole glass. This means all sorts of things can be dealt with in something other than a stressful, emotional-reaction way. For meditation should prepare you to do two things in a tight spot: first, look at your situation and your thoughts and feelings about it objectively, from outside, as if watching a show, just as in meditation you watch thoughts arise and fall; and second, to find a condition of mind which, like the mind in good meditation, is alert, supple, and joyous on the deepest level whatever happens.

Meditation will not only bring you peace of mind. It will also deliver the powerful, and sometimes disturbing, tool of profound self-knowledge if you let it. The "wandering thoughts" that inevitably come and go as you settle into meditation (and sometimes never really leave you alone) are not just random thoughts—they can be vital clues to memories, dreams, fantasies, desires, and fears just under the horizon of consciousness. Like the content of sleeping dreams, they may be the symbol or the "tip of the iceberg" of powerful unconscious forces driving your life. Your fantasies can tell you what you really want and what kind of person you really think you are, now and potentially; that will give you clues to how you will act in a situation that seems to enhance or thwart your desires and your self-image.

Even more significantly, the meditation experience will tell you how you will respond "out there" to such things as frustration, pain, inability to be in control. Meditation is not withdrawal from life: it *is* life, life in a miniaturization in which crucial aspects of it can be experienced, as it were, on a test-case basis.

Suppose, for example, your mind will not go where you want it to. Instead of reaching the Quiet, you can't get out from under worries, imagination, memories that bring chuckles or tears. Do you get angry or upset, trying to force your mind to go the way you wish? Or do you become depressed and feel you're just a failure? Or is it your way to take these things in stride and try to make something creative out of them? Whatever the answer is, the chances are you handle frustrations elsewhere—at work, in family life, with friends—in essentially the same way, and that by carefully observing and analyzing how you respond in meditation you could learn a lot that might be very useful about yourself in all spheres of life.

What about pain? Serious meditation can sometimes be painful. Not only can you get unbearably fidgety or bored, but if you really try to master a classic posture like the lotus you can suffer excruciating pain in the legs and back. As we have said before, it is not necessary that you adopt a posture which entails physical discomfort or pain, but if you bravely elect to do so, you will find that pain in meditation, too, can be a teacher. There is much you can learn about pain, and about yourself, in this way. You will find that even intense pain is not constant but comes and goes, largely in relation to how your consciousness is focused on it. There are many attitudes one can have toward pain, ranging from self-pity through stoic endurance to a strange kind of enjoyment of it. When pain is felt amidst the bright self-awareness of meditation, you will gain insight into your attitudes and what happens if you try to change an attitude.

Looked at this way, there is really no such thing as a bad meditation. In every case, even when the mind seems as uncontrollable as wild horses and the tedium or pain is in full gallop, you can learn much about yourself; indeed, you may come to feel those meditations are more valuable for the other parts of your life than the "good" ones.

As for the alert, supple, and joyous condition of mind which meditation ought to infuse into your daily life, it fits in well with what we have just been talking about. This is precisely the attitude which is deterred by nothing, gains insight from everything, *and* allows each situation to find its own special good. Then one is like the sapling which, though bent, springs back upright; the water which, though diverted, keeps flowing toward the sea, gradually wearing away all barriers to its course; the grass which, though cut, comes up again if its roots are kept moist.

Suppose someone criticizes you abusively and unfairly. The usual reaction is either to lash back with as good as you got, or to be overcome with depression and pull out, maybe in tears. But imagine a person who had learned from meditation experience of out-of-control situations how he or she would respond to them ordinarily, and that the usual response of anger or depression does not do much good. This person should also remember from meditation how to get into the position of observer, not only of the situation as a whole but also of his or her own feelings of anger or depression. The feelings would be there—nothing wrong with feelings *being there*, they're natural—but also there would be a sort of observation/command post above the fray which is in touch with deep joy, never really loses it, and prepares an immediate comeback. The comeback, depending on circumstances, would probably be either a mild but definite rebuke putting the accuser in his/her place, or the kind of laughing, loving reply giving blessing for a curse, which the New Testament calls heaping coals of fire on an adversary's head. Either way, *this* kind of response will establish, and demonstrate, a deep strength far more powerful than rage or tears, one that will resolve the situation as well as can be, and even more important preserve one's own calm joy.

Now about putting meditation to work against specific problems. Say you have an addiction, as for smoking, drinking, or "recreational" drugs, that you know you ought to get under control or eliminate from your life entirely. The addiction is potentially or actually damaging to your health and may be affecting your ability to concentrate or remember. It may be affecting your work life adversely by contributing to absenteeism or an undue need to make money by any means to support the habit. And you spend too much time planning the next cigarette break, drink, or toke in your mind and get anxious if good quantities of the right substances aren't at hand.

It's not easy to break an "adult" habit like this. We can think of a million rationalizations for it. We can always think of people who are worse off than us from the use of tobacco, alcohol, or drugs to reassure us we are doing it responsibly. We can say the strain of quitting would do us more harm. Only *you* can tell whether you have a problem, short of being told so by a doctor or a loved one who knows and cares. But if, after thorough and honest assessment, you decide you do and you want to make a change, meditation can help come to the rescue.

First, it can help you get to know your problem. The self-awareness that meditative introspection produces, which we have already discussed in connection with wandering thoughts and pain, should make you more perceptive about how your mind works, what its dependencies are, and when it is not clear. The alertness, suppleness, and natural joy of meditation will carry over into daily life, and you will become very conscious of when you don't have *that* and are depending on something else instead. If you have ever tried to meditate drunk or stoned, you will know what I mean—you may have a dull kind of calm or even a reeling high, but it's very far from the alert, subtle joy of real meditation, and you will register the difference. So also will you know the difference between the pseudo-euphoria of seeing things under the influence and the "natural high" of seeing them precisely, just as they are, in all their nuances of being and color, that you feel when you look out at the world right after good meditation.

Meditation, then, will help to make you aware of the problem and get a handle on it by showing you that the natural mind, unassisted by any of these crutches, can be as great a turn-on as you could wish. Most people who meditate seriously are either nonusers, or very moderate users, of these substances. Usually they are not into any big crusade against them or highly judgmental of heavier users, though they may be concerned for their well-being. The spirit of meditation teaches a non-extremist, un-dogmatic, sensitive mindset which would not likely produce a Carrie Nation, unless it got way off the track. But at the same time, it produces a mind which simply does not *need* such dependencies; meditators report that once they really get going with medita-tion, the appetite for such things just fades away. Without having to come to any big crisis over it, they simply are smoking, drinking, or taking drugs much less if at all.

Sometimes, of course, it's much less easy, especially if the habit is deeply ingrained or if there is considerable social pressure. In some instances meditation alone is not enough, and the individual ought to seek outside help; that's advisable, and medita-tion will still vigorously support whatever program is undertaken. But there are also ways meditation can be used directly against the habit.

Set your time of meditation right at the time you customarily indulge the habit, when you "really need" a smoke or a drink and normally have one or more, even if that means several times a day. Use very positive supports, visual or auditory, in the meditation to keep the mind strongly focused, and keep meditating until well after the appetite has peaked. If you can get by the times those appetites normally peak, you'll usually be o.k. But if they come back, start meditating again. Even in a social situation, if you know you must abstain, meditate inwardly as you decline politely.

Here is another idea. When you meditate, use as a visual focus some object that represents a higher, purer form of the essential nature of the thing you are trying to overcome: a candle flame for smoking, a bowl or glass of crystal clear water for alcohol, something comparable for the particular kind of drug involved. (The candle is a common focus, and there is a Korean religion which places a bowl of clear water on its altars as a token of the original purity of heaven and the human soul.) Let these pure, passive images replace the sensuous ones which lead to undesired indulgence. For all appetites are first of all actually *appetites in the mind* for images created by habit or outside stimulation; they are acted upon only after the mind-image has arisen. Break the mental pattern with a substitute image, and the chain of habit will begin to wear down.

Of course, the "big three" of smoking, drinking, and drugs are far from the only baneful dependencies. Overeating, sugar, colas, coffee and tea can also become habitual dependencies and can also lead to serious health and attitudinal problems. The same kind of two-pronged counterattack suggested for the former—a general tuning-up of mental condition and specific meditation at difficult times—can also be followed with the help of meditation to get rid of them.

Now let's think about some positive helpmates of meditation for the other parts of your life. Meditation and exercise go together like bread and butter. Exercise such as calisthenics, jogging, swimming, handball, or even strenuous housework or gardening can be a good prelude to meditation, and an equally effective aftermath. It is not without reason that traditional monastic disciplines commonly give balanced attention to meditation and manual labor. When you meditate after a spate of exercise, you will probably find that, although it may take a brief period for the mind and body to settle down from that stimulating activity, soon a deep natural relaxation will come over you that is an excellent foundation for meditative focus. When you meditate and then get up to exercise, the quiet physical toning and mental clarity of the meditation state ought to release like a highly tuned coiled spring to let you bound into exercise activity with tremendous zest. You ought to find yourself flying with a holy joy that is really a continuation of the meditation rather than its postlude; the activity itself, the running, swimming, whatever, is the focus in just the

same way that the candle or still posture is in
the other kind of meditation.

Try to keep it that way. Hold your mind
focused lightly on the here and now of what
the body is doing. If you had a good experience in the seated meditation, hold it in
mind as well. If you use a silent mantra or
chant in meditation, keep it going steadily as
you exercise. If you do koan work, sustain
it.

Remember the importance of slow, deep
breathing for meditative calm, and maintain
it during the exercise. For best meditation
results, the exercise or work should be of a
sort that produces steady, sustained but not
excruciatingly hard exertion, allowing deep
steady breathing without making you
winded and without tension—jogging rather
than the hundred yard dash, hoeing the
garden but not moving pianos.

Yoga postures, of course, are one form of
exercise traditionally associated with
meditation. In India the asanas or postures
and pranayama or breath-control (or control
of the prana or life-energy) are a preliminary

to withdrawal of the attention from outward things before the practice of raja yoga, deep meditation. Yogic postures and breathing go together splendidly, in their combination of muscular tension as one gets into a difficult pose, holds it with still attention, and then relaxes out of it. This tunes up the body and prepares the mind for meditation. Yoga can indeed be a royal road to health and spiritual depth.

We cannot, however, give detailed instruction on the practice of yoga here. If you want to explore this tradition, plenty of other books are available. The best thing to do, though, is to take a yoga class from a qualified instructor; the right practice of yoga is hard to "get" without seeing it demonstrated and practicing it under personal guidance. On a more intangible level, the charisma of a good yoga teacher and the relaxing, supportive atmosphere of a class are assets hard to duplicate.

Besides exercise and yoga, there are other activities that consort well with meditation. These include music, games, and study. Here again, the meditation can be either before or after, or even both, with a different effect in each case. Meditating before practice, playing music—whether practicing, recreational, performance playing or singing—will reduce tension and help to open up the inner fountains of expression and intuitive grasp so important to a great performance. It can also help the mind clarify itself and focus so that it is conscious only of what it is doing now and prepared to put all its attention on the playing.

To meditate before playing a game, be it baseball or chess, championship play or strictly for fun, can have much the same benefit. Here, too, it reduces tension and strengthens attention and the capacity for swift intuitive insight into what needs to be done. It should also make playing the game more fun. As in exercise, you should get up from the meditation with an eager, zestful spirit that wants to get out there, enjoy the playfulness of the game, and win. It should give you that special inner rhythm and equilibrium that makes you and the game a part of each other and makes you just *know* what to do in each situation, even when there's no time to think.

Time to think is what you have when you're studying, though. You may be going to school and have papers to write and exams to prepare for. You may be trying to keep up with your profession or business. Or you may be learning a foreign language or computer programming on your own. Whatever it is, try meditating, if only for a few minutes, before you begin.

When you meditate after something like music, games, or study, this serves as a seal to concentrate and hold in the essence of the experience. It pulls together and helps your psyche utilize the soaring or tranquil exaltation of the music, leaving you one with it on some deep level. It brings you down from the high of the game, helps you to accept calmly the win or loss, while sealing in its joy and transmuting its energy to refreshing rest. After study, you will find meditation will help you to crystallize in your mind the key points of the material so that they are well retained and understood.

Now we shall look at how meditation impacts on some other areas of life. Take family life. Those of us who live in families—who have to get along with parents, brothers, and sisters, or who have the joys, headaches, and heartaches of our own marriages and children—know that families can be the most happy and the most frustrating, if not downright destructive, of all human environments. They can support you like a featherbed and slice you up like a chainsaw. They can bring out your best and your worst, give you deep love and unbearable tension.

That's because in families relationships are largely given; you pretty much have to take what you get. You may choose your own spouse—though even this is more of a shot in the dark than we often like to admit, since fickle fate so much determines who we meet at the right time and place, and where the arrow of Cupid lands. Furthermore, people change, and no one knows till twenty years after the wedding bells what it's like to be married to someone for twenty years. You don't choose your parents, unless in some other world, and you don't choose your children. Yet it's impossible to get out of these relations, or at least difficult without terrible pain and guilt. However much children may send them up the wall, most parents know they cannot abandon their children; and however incompatible, children find it very hard not to see their relationships with their parents as very important, so much is it wound around one's psyche from earliest infancy.

In the warm, intricate nest of family relationships, meditation can help in two ways. It can provide a countervailing sense of identity apart from family, and it can provide a "tranquillity base" from which to deal with the bad times.

First the sense of personal identity. At times it is important to know you are not *just* the person your parents made you or want you to be, or *just* a supporting servant of your spouse or children. You are not only your place in the family relationship chart. While there can be couple and group meditation, it is most often done alone and when family relations are a point of tension, it should be. Family meditation, like family prayer, can enrich and strengthen a good relationship that is already there, but it will not usually solve problems that cut deep. It may only exacerbate them for some members, since an expectation that one participate in family prayer or meditation is likely to appear, to a person basically alienated from the family, as an exercise of familial authoritarianism trying to override one's individuality. Better for people to get themselves together first with the help of private meditation and—if it is in the cards—feel better about the family as a result. (We will discuss meditating with others in the next chapter.)

Meditating alone is as highly private, personal, individual an act as is possible. It affords contact with that which is most substantial yet most personal in you, the foundation of your own consciousness—and if you wish, is your own personal link with eternal, Ultimate Reality.

When you are in meditation, you are just yourself, you are experiencing yourself, sensing yourself, knowing yourself. You can arise from meditation with an inner joy and verve no one can take from you. When the family stress level gets high, then meditate and find yourself at the deepest stratum of joy and peace, where you are a separate person, a real person, a valuable person, quite apart from the family nexus. It doesn't matter what anyone says, it doesn't matter whether you meet anyone else's expectations concerning you and what you do or don't do. You are still the person with the depth and reality you know yourself to have in meditation. Better yet, meditate regularly so that you always have that reserve available when the family going is tough.

Then it becomes not only a source of affirmative personal identity apart from that stuck on you by family, but also a base of joyful strength. . . for joy is strength and strength is joy. Have you ever noticed that when you're really happy you can handle almost anything? Meditation gives that joy by first giving deep peace and calm. When a person is truly calm, joy—even euphoria—wells up of its own in a normal healthy individual.

When astronauts first landed on the moon in 1969, their base of operations, since it was in the lunar Sea of Tranquillity, was called "tranquillity base." This is a good way to think of your meditation time and place, as your own tranquillity base in the midst of stormy scenes, if so it be. Let it infuse into your life the inner joy which rides out nearly any typhoon.

Family problems and stormy living room scenes are not, of course, the only place where unbearable stress arises, nor are the times parents feel they just cannot cope with

being awakened one more time by a crying
infant, or settling one more quarrel between
vengeful siblings. There are also work and
one's network of friends and associates. The
seamy side of both these sets can induce
powerful stress. In business, anxiety over
how things are going, the constant need to
make a good impression, the fundamental
tedium of most jobs, the depressing pettiness
of office politics, can grind one down to the
hard core or beyond.

Once again, we don't pretend that meditation is a panacea that will automatically
solve all problems. Nor will it magically
resolve the tangled yarn of friendly relations, snarled with jealousies and misunderstandings, hurt feelings and even tears
—especially when romance and eros may
be involved.

But meditation can offer some tools in ad-
dition to providing a tranquillity base and
the assurance that you as an individual are
real and important. In work and friendship
problems, meditating *for* and, under the

right circumstances, *with* another can be powerfully effective. This may be a little too heavy for family problems, but may be just right for people you didn't grow up with or don't live with all the time.

In meditating for someone, just hold an image of the person in mind as you meditate—or look at a picture of the person—using the individual as your focus. Try not to think consciously about the problems or prospects regarding the person. Just visualize the person as you enter the Quiet Mind, and if you think of anything, think the same reality you reach in meditation, whatever you call it, is in that person. Whatever the nature of the relationship, you will find that afterwards you will never again be able to think of that person in quite the same way as before, and will probably see something better, something more positive in him and in the relationship. Whether or not things go better in regard to the person in the "real" world, it should not bother you quite so much. The level of resentment will go down and the love and affirmation toward him will be enhanced, improving your own peace of mind—even if what you feel is unspoken, even if you are rightly unable to approve of what he or she did or does, even if you are very willing that your paths no longer cross. As an exercise in "loving your enemies," you could sometime try meditating for those whom you feel to be the worst people, both in your own life and in the world. It may do both you and them some good. (We will talk more about meditating for others in the next chapter.)

You can meditate with a person with whom you have a special relation, whether good or problematic, in either of two ways. Meditate as it were side by side, in the same place, but without direct looking or physical contact, so that you just share the same atmosphere of peace; or meditate alone with a mental image of the other as the actual focus, so that you are really using the other to bring you to God or Ultimate Reality, and communicating that power to the one you are thinking of. This is interpersonal meditation, the topic of the next chapter.

7

Interpersonal Meditation

If you think of meditation as an intensely and relentlessly private act, like reading a book only more so, you will not be very different on this score from most people. So it usually is. In this volume we have generally approached meditation that way, except at the very end of the preceeding chapter. We have, in fact, seen how meditation alone—finding time to be yourself with yourself—in the midst of social faces and social places can help you be a real person in

128

the whirlwind of pressures to be what others want you to be. It can be a way to drop down a magic rejuvenating rabbit-hole once in a while in the thick of family or social hassles.

And if you think that meditation is at the opposite pole on some inner axis from the strong human feelings we often associate with interpersonal relationships—especially when they become much more than mere business connections or casual acquaintances but instead are the kind that wind up your feelings and get you deeply involved in other lives—again you will not be far from the impression most people have. Meditation is thought to be calm and "spiritual," emotional relationships to be "human" and distinctly unspiritual. Those passions easily fly out of control or become self-indulgent, while meditation lifts us to "higher things."

Again, there is truth to the common assumptions. Heavy interpersonal involvement can unquestionably lead to billowing turbulence that is destructive in one's own life and that of others, like unrestrained appetite for food and drink. You worry inordinately about such things as, What does the other person think of me? Why do we quarrel when we really don't want to? Why does he / she bring out the best and worst in me? Above all, why is the relationship just so blasted *important* to me when I know, ideally, that spiritual life is much more vital? But, we tell ourselves, I'm just not a person who can always live in eternity. I feel confused because emotional involvements pull me two ways, making me feel both authentic and inauthentic at the same time. I sense in these intense relationships something that is really me coming out, and yet I also sense putting on an unreal social mask and running through emotional changes like someone had turned on the machinery.

Then there are those of us who are afraid of intense involvements with other people altogether, or at least very reluctant to essay them. We'd rather just keep to ourselves. Yet there are times when, despite that bent, we feel a dry, empty yearning inside, a sense something bright and glorious *could* happen to us if we could just let it, perhaps even some new way of experiencing Ultimate Reality through human face and form. We don't know which side of us is most real, but in spite of some wistfulness we're inclined to sink into Sloth or Cow routines with our aloneness.

Of course, some people are called to hidden lives of much solitude for the best of reasons, among them some of the monks, nuns, saints, and mystics of all religions. Their roster includes certain of the greatest and most authentically human men and women the world has known. But they were drawn to the hidden life by something far higher than fear. Too often, if we abstain from interpersonal life, it is only out of fear—fear of getting involved, fear of being hurt, fear of anything that will upset a comfortable routine.

Interpersonal meditation can help with both situations. It can make interpersonal relations that exist more authentic, and it can help to overcome fear when fear is the main reason one does not have them. In both cases it can help make interpersonal relations, not a distraction to the spiritual life, but a real means of spiritual growth.

By interpersonal meditation we do not now mean meditation *for* the other, or private meditation to help you stabilize yourself in the thick of difficult interpersonal situations, but meditation *with* the other. The other person himself or herself becomes the meditation focus, and the purpose is to experience the infinity, the joy, the authenticity, that is at the center of that person, as it is in your own center and that of all creation. For what could be more real than a relationship based on such common deep-leveled oneness?

We must never forget that the target reality of meditation—God, infinite being, mental calm—is not *only* to be found within oneself. It may be there, and it may all be latent there. But we humans are not made to find everything in ourselves and learn everything afresh by ourselves as though no other humans existed or had ever existed.

We have language, and we have relations with others, beginning with parents. God, reality, comes as messages from without as well as upwellings within. This is good, for it helps us to realize our dependence on that which is outside of ourselves—other persons, the world, the infinite universe. We are each part of an endless circuit of energy and knowing, each of us single mirrors in an unbounded hall of mirrors, reflecting and energizing one another, knowing the self in the other and the other in the self. This is love, fully to accept and rejoice in that ongoing flow, whether generally or in the particular persons with whom we have special relationships. Unlove is to try to hold the light and begrudge the flow, to try to pull back from one's place in the eternal play of the world's energy / knowledge system. It

brings death, for no life can long live wholly
by itself, either physically or spiritually. We
are meant to live for each other, and life is an
electricity that fails unless it is wired in a
complete circuit through many lives.

Interpersonal meditation, or love meditation, then, counters the great spiritual
demon which is likely to dog those following
the meditation path, narcissism. The Greek
youth Narcissus for whom this evil is named
fell so much in love with himself, in the form
of his own reflection, that he pined away.
Narcissism is self-love in the form of excessive preoccupation with one's own inner
feelings and a corresponding inability to
take the reality of others seriously. The nar-
cissist's only concern, even in interpersonal
situations, is whether he or she is really "self-
fulfilled" in the relation, not whether life-
energy and knowledge are being exchanged.

Interpersonal meditation clears you to
know that the light in yourself shines in

others as well and can shine *for you* in another. It teaches powerfully that good meditation means, not obsession with inner "states," but simply an open, receiving attitude, willing to learn and grow through another. Precisely the same attitudes are needed to love well, or even just to get along. So meditation can upbuild love, even as love strengthens meditation.

The meditation we are talking about now is based on the special relations which come naturally between persons, whether couples, parents and children, or intimate friends. Some few such as the saints and mystics of whom we have spoken may be able to experience the universal energy / knowledge system equally in everyone, and so have transcended the need for special relationships. But for most of us that is too much to handle, and we know it most through particularized energy / knowledge systems in which we are acutely involved, embracing persons with complementary energies and knowledges.

Let's look at meditation between two adults. Perhaps they are male and female in love. Love is one of those words we use constantly, but which, if we are ever pressed to define exactly what we mean by it, proves remarkably hard to pin down. This is not the place for an exhaustive treatment of the definition. But certainly, when it characterizes a particularized adult relationship, it has some special qualities. There is a felt need for the other to be present to complete something big in one's one life, a sense of physical and mental attractiveness in the other which you want to see and experience often, and a sense that some dimension of life you do not have is *given* you through the other. Besides this, there is an awareness of common destiny, that you are going to go through major parts of your lives together. It may be, in the words of the traditional marriage ceremony, "for richer, for poorer; for better, for worse," but the common destiny is *there*.

All these aspects are enriched by interpersonal meditation. The basic idea is very simple. Be together, feel together the love or deep friendship of the relation, let the other person be the one-pointed focus to stop the action, so that the Quiet Mind is quiet on, with, and in that other person. Presumably he or she will be reaching the same place with you at the same time.

Remember part of the point is to know and experience the other, and the divine in the other, more deeply. So don't hesitate to focus on that which is most endearing about the other person to you. Everyone who is really *known* has some special "look" or mood or feature, some "certain smile," which seems mysteriously to sum up that individual's charm and personality. It may even, for those profoundly in love, do what Beatrice did to Dante that caused him to write of her, "her least salutation / bestows salvation on this favored one/and humbles him till he forgets all wrongs." Even if you see that smile only once a week or so, when you see it the real person shines through, and you treasure most those photographs which capture it, saying this is "really" the one I love. In interpersonal meditation, bring out and fix your gaze on that smile or that special feature.

It can be the same between parent and child. What more crucial or profound exchange of energy and knowledge is there than this? Meditate looking at a new baby deep in the cradle, or an older child asleep on the pillow. That will be an incredibly rich focus for appreciation with contemplative awe, the ever renewing life and mind of the universe. In the midst of all the hassles of parenting, we need to take time out simply to know the sacred being at the center of all the tumult and the shouting.

Or interpersonal meditation can be done with friends, when the overtones of love and family are not necessarily part of the picture, but when two, or a few, people are on the same wave-length spiritually and can meditate together creatively. Focusing on one another if the explicit intention is interpersonal meditation, let them know each other as light-bearer, life-bearer, and God-bearer.

We are physical/spiritual beings in whom spirit is hidden in concealing and revealing clouds of flesh, like a sun behind multi-shaped and multi-colored banks of sunrise, its own clear light seen only as it tints and forms those morning fogs. In interpersonal meditation, then, look for the spiritual sun rising in the other person; see it shine till it breaks clear; yet also let the other's unique face and form delicately lens it in a special way, for each person's refracting of the light is a gift to the world never seen before and never to come again. If it is not appreciated, or if darkened, eons will be the poorer by so much.

During meditation, also visualize the transfer of energy between the two or around the group. See streams of life and power glancing fast as light and strong as dynamos between faces and hands. This energy is like a personalized expression, filtered though the personality of each person, of the universal life-energy which mysteriously animates all things, and which is also the universal love-energy which binds all things together in a network of mutual dependence. The ethical expression of accepting this network is loving, knowing, caring, finding one's life in others.

Finally formal interpersonal meditation comes to an end. It should not, in fact, be allowed to drag out into greater and greater dissipation of intensity and energy. Better to end while people are still reasonably "warm." Then the meditation will be carried forward on another level through the rest of the day and night—in a special glow in the eye whenever the participants happen to look at each other again, in a special spark, maybe a special hug, when they meet after absence, in a special happy sense of lightness and energy in the relationship.

8

Meditating for Others

Love is a many-splendored thing which can be expressed in diverse ways. Not only can love meditation enhance love; it can also generate and direct energy to those in need, whether in body or spirit—and who is not in need in some way? Who would not benefit from the meditative love of someone else?

In this chapter we shall discuss three ways of meditating for others: first, private meditation for others, thinking of them while meditating alone, a practice rather like prayer; second, meditating in the presence of another who is troubled; and third, meditating to create a calm and energized state of mind in preparation for spiritual healing through the laying-on-of-hands.

It must be emphasized that no special quasi-magical power is claimed for these practices. Those who believe in prayer can think of them as meditative forms of prayer. Those who believe that love or "good vibes" can be sent people over the airwaves or through the "therapeutic touch" of healing hands can think of them as ways of doing that. Those for whom all such concepts are difficult but who are full of good will toward others can think of them as simply ways of building up those sentiments when alone, or showing that you care enough just to be quiet with another who is sick or disturbed when in his or her presence. Once again, it is not our concern to promote any theology or theory of meditation, but to show that it can be of great value to individuals within the contexts of differing world views.

Many people, when meditating alone, like to meditate for others, both people they love and people they know to be in need. This can be thought of as directing energy to the person, just as in love meditation, previously discussed, except that here the other is absent and it is more of a one-way sending. (Of course, two people separated from each other can meditate and send back and forth at the same time—even, with a little figuring, across many time zones.)

You can focus on the person as you would on any focus. Create an internal image of the person in your mind or, if it helps, don't hesitate to use a picture or a token of the person such as a lock of hair. Then, just hold the person quietly in the light and calm of your meditative Quiet Mind. Then, as you go more deeply into meditation, let your focus be a great pool of light and warmth in the center of your being—in your heart or that spiritual center which some say is in the area of the solar plexus, just above the navel.

Visualize this light spreading healing energy throughout the body of the other. If he or she is in need, see and feel it going especially to parts of the body and soul requiring healing. Hold that person in the light.

Meditation for another by either method need not be excessively prolonged. Those who feel drawn to meditate regularly for several people often devote about ten minutes to each, going from one to another.

Meditation for others can, of course, be done very effectively by a group. Under the verbal direction of a leader, or silently if the members are experienced, groups can hold someone else in the light. Meditating in unison results in a strong sense of concentrating power.

Sometimes you may want to meditate for another person with that person actually present. This is different from the interpersonal meditation of the previous chapter since that practice assumes the two are more or less equal in energy and are sharing knowledge and power with one another.

Now we are talking about a situation in which, while there is caring, there is not necessarily special love between the persons, and in which one is in need of help from another. Use this meditation, of course, only with a person who really wants it and feels comfortable with it.

If possible, sit in your best meditation posture facing the other person, who should be in a somewhat similar position and at the same height as you. Of course, if the other person is sick in bed or is much more comfortable seated in a chair, you must adjust. Whether you meditate standing, seated, or in a lotus position on the floor, it is important that you be at about the same level as the other person, have good eye contact with him or her, and that neither of you feels any strain. If you want to hold hands, that's fine.

Settle into the Quiet Mind, using a mantra if you wish, and focus on the other person—not with a penetrating stare, but with a calm awareness. Visualize yourself as filling with warm light and sending it through your eyes and hands to the other person. Or simply visualize the other person as filling with the same warm light, welling up from inner sources of purity and strength, from the grace of God touching him or her deep within. Hold the other person in the light this way for some ten or fifteen minutes, always exuding light, calm, and healing love.

It might be added that hurt or distraught animals, too, often respond dramatically to this sort of meditation. They are highly sensitive to the mental state of humans around them, and just as fear or anger or anxiety in people will call up corresponding negative behavior in animals, so the confident calm of a person in meditation will frequently lead them to a comparable state.

Meditation for another who is present leads easily to reflection on healing and meditation. Spiritual healing is most commonly done through the biblical practice of the laying-on-of-hands, either on the person's head or the afflicted part. It may also be done by holding the hand slightly cupped, like a lens, above the person, or with "passes" through the air above the sick individual, or by verbal commands or concentration, and other means. It is not intended to replace the physician's art, but to support it by—if one wish—imparting healing energy and, above all, by helping the sick person find a state of mind conducive to recovering health. Many doctors, aware through long experience of how important belief and mental condition are to recovery, and of how mysterious the healing process can actually be, are more than willing for such techniques to be used in conjunction with medicine.

We will concentrate on the laying-on-of-hands. In our view, such practices are not magic or raw "faith," but an extension of meditation, and especially of meditating with and for another. It is meditating for another in need, sick in mind or body, while gently but securely using one's hands as a channel and token of caring love.

Touching can be important. True, culture has sometimes put taboos on touching—it must not be done in public, it must be done only between people of certain degrees of relationship, and so forth. But children, with their untrammeled instincts, know how important it is. Unless they have been severely wronged, they naturally want to touch and play with those whom they love. Infants who are never held or fondled languish and may even die. There is something of the infant and child still in all of us, and especially when we are sick or troubled, a caring touch can still, in the proverbial phrase, work wonders. It can convey, in a direct way words never quite can, that one is still part of the network of life, that people are reaching out and want you to know it in every possible way.

Here, then, is the occasion for combining the virtues of meditation with those of touching. Let the person being touched know it. Touch with love, almost with a caress, yet also with a sense of power and authority. Then let your meditation match the touch. Work for clarity and a sense of power for good in the mind. Let your focus be the hands themselves, and see benign luminous energy streaming through them. Very often healers report a definite heat develops in the hands during the exercise. Visualize the afflicted limb or organ fill with light and become as whole and healthy as it once was and can be again. Finally, behold the entire person in the light, seeing that person hale and radiant as he or she was meant to be. Throughout the exercise you may pray or recite a mantra quietly, whatever seems right to you. The prayer-mantra "Let thy Light shine through me" is a very appropriate and effective one.

Persons receiving healing meditation with the laying-on-of-hands will frequently comment that they feel much better. This is, of course, wonderful, but it should not be interpreted as a medical change (though that may be an eventual result) so much as the good feeling that warmth, touching, and calm almost always bring. A close acquaintance of mine who often does this kind of healing told me of laying hands with meditation on the head of a friend who had suffered from a terrible headache for three days. The pain immediately went away. It came back awhile later, however, suggesting that the laying-on-of-hands had affected a temporary calming of whatever tension or affliction was causing the headache, rather than a permanent healing. But, of course, any relief of pain is a blessed thing and can create psychological conditions for more lasting improvement, so long as proper medical attention is also sought. On another occasion involving the same two persons, the patient was feverish and suffering from nausea. The healer laid hands on the stomach, chest, and neck. This time the patient said that the hands felt cool, rather than hot as usual, as if they were to calm and bring down the fever. The patient soon got up, feeling much better.

Once again, though, let us emphasize that physical contact is not necessary to healing meditation, even when healer and receiver are together. Some receivers may prefer not to be touched; if so, those feelings must be respected. The giver can channel the light by holding the hand several inches away from the receiver's body, or even just by meditating inwardly. The calm strength of the meditation is what counts.

The greatest benefit of healing meditation, as of all meditation for others, is the effect it works on the minds and souls of giver and receiver alike. It teaches receivers to know that they are loved and cared for, and it teaches givers to love and care. You will find that it is difficult if not impossible for you to hate someone after you have meditated for that person. Instead, after meditating for someone or offering that person healing, you will discover yourself seeing good where you didn't before, and the relation may become warmer in all sorts of ways. Meditation works for healing in whatever lives it touches.

9

Getting It Together

The Quiet Mind, we have seen, is the mind taking time out just to be itself—not the Monkey Mind, the Sloth Mind, or the Cow Mind with all their sad games. We have surveyed how to come to the Quiet Mind, how to experience it, and what to do with it. The rest is up to you.

Put into practice, meditation may have a radical impact on your life. Be prepared for this. It will be not only a practice but a subtle force that could well reorder your values and priorities.

The word *radical* comes from the Latin term for *root*, and meditation is a radical practice in the sense that it operates at the roots of your being. It allows you to uncover and experience a level of your being—or of universal being—that the game levels cover over. When you have experienced something other than the games of consciousness you can never be the same again.

You will have, probably, some new values. You will know there is something real and deeply joyous which can be neither bought nor sold and which no one else can take from you. It is entirely apart from the worlds of money, of competition, of getting ahead or falling behind, of human loves and hates, worlds which we are often tempted to think are all there is, so noisy and boisterous do they appear. Realizing the Something Else known in meditation immediately puts a new and revealing light on all their houses of cards. You will find you have a choice about how important money is to you, how much you want to compete, how much you cling to others, what is really important to you.

In other words, with your new Secret Resource, you can take more real charge of your own life.

Other upshots might be more disturbing, at least at first. The experience of meditation may also lead you to ask far-reaching questions. You may question what you once took for granted, not only in life-values, but also in religion and philosophy. What kind of a universe *is* it, and what kind of a creature is a human being, that meditation can be so significant within them?

You may also find yourself more creative. Meditation can open up levels of mind from which ideas and inspirations can come, but which a humdrum life of Monkey, Sloth, or Cow mentality seals over. You may find ideas popping up for anything from a new product to a new song to a new way of looking at life and people. This may sound great, and it is, but when a person who has settled into a comfortable routine as a run-of-the-mill bank teller or barber suddenly develops an overwhelming need to paint or write poetry, it can be unsettling, to say the least, to that person and the family as well. All I can say is, be ready for changes.

But if you're one of those people who agree that a rainbow is better than gray overcast and is worth a summer shower, go try it. Take up meditation and see what happens.

QUEST BOOKS

are published by
The Theosophical Society in America,
a branch of a world organization
dedicated to the promotion of brotherhood and
the encouragement of the study of religion,
philosophy, and science to the end that man may
better understand himself and his place in
the universe. The Society stands for complete
freedom of individual search and belief.
In the Theosophical Classics Series
well-known occult works are made
available in popular editions.